ALL ABOUT CRUISES tells you everything you need to know about taking a cruise: information on cruise lines, their ships, prices, and vacations to more than 500 destinations around the world. It tells you what to pack, what to wear, what to expect, and how to get the best deals.

ALL ABOUT CRUISES takes you from the time you decide to take a cruise until after the cruise when you arrive at your front door. It takes you through the entire procedure, step by step, to insure your safety and enjoyment.

ALL ABOUT CRUISES explains why cruising is the only way to go! Compared to most land-based vacations it is oftentimes not only **less expensive** but you get to see so very much more. And there's no hassle; you pack and unpack but one time. Your "hotel on the sea" is your home for your entire vacation. It travels with you.

ALL ABOUT CRUISES tells the wide choices of continuous entertainment that is included in the price of your vacation. And the food, Ahh! That is yet another thing. You'll eat the types of food most people only dream of—about a dozen times a day. Each evening you dress, stroll just a short way to your exquisite dinner and entertainment and stroll back. What a vacation!

ALL ABOUT CRUISES

by

SHIRLEY RAGUSA
and
PETE BILLAC

Swan Publishing
New York●California●Texas

Authors: Shirley Ragusa and Pete Billac
Cover Designer: Shelby Berry
Layout Design: Sharon Davis
Cover photo: The Crystal Harmony, Courtesy of Crystal Cruises

Other Books by Pete Billac:

The Anninihilator
How Not to Be Lonely
The Last Medal of Honor
How Not to Be Lonely—TONIGHT
New Father's Baby Guide

Copyright @ August 1996
Shirley Ragusa, Pete Billac and SWAN Publishing
Library of Congress #96-68889
ISBN# 0-943629-23-3

ALL ABOUT CRUISES is available in quantity discounts through SWAN Publishing, 126 Live Oak, Alvin, TX 77511. (713)388-2547 or FAX (713)585-3738.

Printed in the United States of America.

Dedication

To the cruise lines,
who are constantly searching for better ways to spoil
and pamper all who cruise with them.
And,
to travel agents and travel agencies. Without your
knowledge, effort, care and patience in dealing with
your customers, there wouldn't be a cruise industry.

ACKNOWLEDGMENTS

A special thanks to the following cruise lines and their public relations departments for their cooperation, photographs, information and updates.

American Hawaii Cruises

Carnival Cruise Lines

Celebrity Cruises

Costa Cruises

Crystal Cruises

Cunard

Holland America/Westours

Norwegian Cruise Lines

Premier Cruise Lines

Princess Cruises

Radisson Seven Seas Cruises

Renaissance Cruises

Royal Caribbean Cruise Line

Royal Olympic Cruises
(Sun Line and Epirotiki)

Seabourn Cruise Lines

SilverSea Cruises

Windstar Cruises

Windjammers

Delta Queen Steamboat Company

INTRODUCTION

This book was written by Shirley Ragusa and Pete Billac, cruise enthusiasts. They visited numerous bookstores looking for a book that told cruisers how to choose the right ship and get the best deal. Then what they need to know to enjoy that cruise to the fullest. They found none to their liking. Because of this, *ALL ABOUT CRUISES* was written.

Pete has taken 63 of these ocean voyages on 14 different cruise lines as of this writing; five were 3-day cruises and the others from one week to one month. Shirley, the coauthor, is a cruise professional. She has cruised with most of the top cruise lines in the world and has her own worldwide cruise consulting service.

Shirley and Pete concur that **regardless** of the ship or destination you choose, you're in for a marvelous time. There are no bad cruises—only different ones and better ones. If this is your 1st or 50th cruise, this book will help you. As they write this book and you read it, there are newer and more fascinating ships being built. They will give you information on those as well as the ones that will suit your every desire and pocketbook.

They have listed the cruise lines that offer luxury cruising at it's finest, as well as others that offer the best price. This is an ample cross-section from which you may choose your next vacation.

There are cruises that last from three days to more than 100 days. There are ships that carry as few as 100 passengers and those that carry over 2,500. There are cruise lines whose ships cater to singles, families, honeymooners, and couples. There are cruises with destinations to the best known vacation spots in the world and cruises that are for those who seek raw adventure and want to travel to those hideaways few people ever go. And cruises for those who can afford the very best.

ALL ABOUT CRUISES is the perfect book for those of you who have never cruised before because you are taken, step by step, through the entire process. It tells you where, when, and how. It helps you pack, tells where to get a passport, and how to select the ship and length of cruise that is perfect for you.

This book tells about the wonderful amenities and activities on the various ships, the way to choose shore excursions, which ones to take and which ones to go on your own. It tells about the food, how to choose traveling companions, insurance, and literally whatever you need to know.

ALL ABOUT CRUISES was reviewed by several cruise experts who feel that it is the *best* book on cruising there is! The authors tried to make it factual, fun, and interesting. Now, let's get into the book. I hope you read it, use it, and enjoy it. There's no doubt you'll benefit from this inside information.

Publisher

TABLE OF CONTENTS

The authors researched the information on cruise lines, their ships, prices and itineraries contained in this book to the best of their ability, based on information in the newspapers, the cruise lines, travel brochures and travel magazines. The prices are subject to change as are the ownership of the ships and cruise lines. Be certain to consult with a professional agent for current dates, itineraries and prices.

Chapter 1

WHY TAKE A CRUISE

Cruising is the most exciting, romantic, marvelous, relaxing, carefree vacation there is. Also, it is more often than not, far less expensive than a land-based vacation! Look at the chart below that we "borrowed" from the CLIA (Cruise Lines International Association) book.

COST COMPARISON

Typical Caribbean Cruise Vacation
VS
Typical Resort Vacation
Based on two adults traveling from St. Louis for 7 nights

	CRUISE VACATION	RESORT VACATION
Base Price	$2,400	$2,008
Airfare	Included	$1,098
Transfers	Included	Included
Meals	Included	$ 805
Tips	$ 105	$ 200
Sightseeing	$ 266	$ 405
Entertainment	Included	$ 160
Beverages	$ 183	$ 264
Souvenirs	$ 100	$ 100
TOTAL	$3,054	$5,040
COST PER DAY	$ 218	$ 360

Actual savings may vary based on vacation choice.

Not a believer? If you're planning a land-based vacation, take out your notebook and jot down the cost of your airline ticket, transfers to and from your hotel, guess on the low side what the cost of meals and entertainment will be, taxis to and from the airport to your hotel, and compare it to the price of any one of the cruises we have listed.

Also, a cruise is so convenient in that you have to make almost *no decisions*—unless you care to. There is continuous entertainment and you have a wide variety of choices. We put in a *Daily Activity* chart so you can see for yourself. This one is three pages long and is for but **one single day!** Such a schedule will be in your cabin each evening listing activities for the following day.

Dining Today

7:00am-10:00am	Eye-Opener Coffee & Cinnamon Rolls	Yacht Club, Deck 7
7:30am-11:00am	Continental Breakfast is available	Staterooms
7:30am-9:30am	BREAKFAST is served-OPEN seating	Dining Room
8:00am-10:00am	BREAKFAST BUFFET	Yacht Club, Deck 7
10:45am-11:15am	Hot Bullion is served	Yacht Club, Deck 7
12:00pm	LUNCHEON is served-MAIN seating	Dining Room
12:00pm-1:30pm	LUNCHEON BUFFET	Yacht Club, Deck 7
12:00pm-1:30pm	Soup, Salad & Sandwiches available	Lido Lounge, Deck8
12:00pm-1:30pm	Grilled specials (weather permitting)	Grill, Deck 10
1:30pm	LUNCHEON is served-LATE seating	Dining Room
4:00-4:45pm	Tea with Cookies, Cakes & Yogurt	Yacht Club, Deck 7
6:30pm (Main)	AROUND THE WORLD DINNER	Dining Room
8:30pm (Late)	AROUND THE WORLD DINNER	Dining Room
11:30pm-12:30am	Late Evening Light Buffet	Yacht Club, Deck 7

■ Fitness Afloat ■

8:00am	SUNRISE AEROBICS—Start the day fit!	Gym, Deck 8
8:45am	*Tummy Tune Up*—Take home a trimmer you.	Gym, Deck 8
10:00am	PERSONAL TRAINING—Bring your fitness questions to Wendi	Gym, Deck 8
10:45am	HIP & WAIST AWAY—Lower body workout designed for women.	Gym, Deck 8
4:00pm	SUNSET AEROBICS—Finish your day feeling fit & refreshed.	Gym, Deck 8
4:45pm	*Tummy Tune Up II*—Exercises that work!	Gym, Deck 8

■ Morning Activities ■

8:30am	DAILY QUIZ—First correct answers before noon wins a prize!	Reception, Deck 5
9:30am	BRIDGE TALK—Join Ross for his next lecture	Penthouse Lounge, Deck 9
9:30am	CRETE PORT TALK—Join port lecturer Frank for his discussion on Heraklion & Crete. This will air simultaneously on Channel 1 (TV) and will be rebroadcast at 6:30pm on Channel 3 (radio).	Palm Lounge, Deck 6
9:45am	NAVIGATIONAL BRIDGE VISIT—Numbers are limited but there will be other tours on this cruise.	Deck 7, Forward
10:15am	FASHION SHOW—Come see the fashions you may have missed in the Boutique! The Ship's staff and entertainers will do the modeling.	Palm Lounge, Deck 6
10:30am	MIXED TABLE TENNIS—Meet up with friends and play for fun!	Poolside, Deck 6
11:00am	SERVICE CLUBS MEETING: Lions, Rotarians, Kiwanians, etc., meet with Jeff. All Club members welcome.	Lido Lounge, Deck 8
11:00am	COUNTRY LINE DANCE—If you are interested in Being part of our Passenger Talent Shows— please meet for a ½ hour practice.	Palm Lounge, Deck 6
11:00am	ICE CARVING DEMONSTRATION: Come and see the artistic talent of ice carving by our expert, Rodolfo (weather permitting)	Poolside, Deck 7
11:15am	PIZZA & BLOODY MARY PARTY—Compliments of the Captain. In the Penthouse Bar, Yacht Club, Lido Lounge, Top of the Crown, & poolside.	Ship's Lounges
12:00pm	TALENT SHOW REGISTRATION—Do you eat fire, swallow swords, sing, dance, tell a story? If so, we need you for the afternoon's Passenger Talent Show. Please meet for rehearsal with Jeff & Craig at the piano.	Palm Lounge

■ Afternoon Activities ■

1:30pm	DUPLICATE & RUBBER BRIDGE—with Jackie	Penthouse Lounge
2:00pm	MIXED SHUFFLEBOARD FUN—Meet with friends & play this popular deck game.	Promenade, Deck 7, Port
2:00pm	NAVIGATIONAL BRIDGE VISIT—Numbers are limited but there will be other tours on this cruise.	Deck 7, Forward
2:00pm	NEW BEGINNINGS—*"Living & Loving Past The Big 5-0"*, is a fun-filled, entertaining & informative topic told by one of America's most sought-after speakers, *Pete Billac*. Pete has written scrips for ALL IN THE FAMILY, M*A*S*H* and BARNEY MILLER. He has appeared on GOOD MORNING AMERICA, SALLY JESSY RAPHAEL, DONAHUE (even Morton Downey, Jr). Join Pete. He'll make you laugh—hard!	Palm Lounge
2:15pm	CHECKERS—Players meet for unsupervised play	Gameroom
2:15pm	INFORMAL CHESS PLAY—Unsupervised.	Gameroom
3:00pm	THE STORY OF THE GREAT SHIPS (Part I)— The first in a series of three lectures by your Cruise Director, Lindsey. The early days of trans-atlantic travel, the first great passenger steam ships, the story of the Mauretania, Lusitania, Titanic and the beautiful Ile de France & many more. Illustrated with a collection of rare slides.	Laguna Theater
4:00pm	MOVIE "THE ROCK" starring Sean Connery and Nicholas Cage.	
4:30pm	$BINGO BONANZA$—Play for the big jackpot of $300 plus lots of cash prizes!	Palm Lounge

---

6:15pm & 9:45pm   Palm Lounge

SHOW TIME
featuring the vocals of
Christopher Carter *in*
"A BITE OF THE BIG APPLE"
followed by the unique talents of
DIANE MARTIN

6-8:00pm   CESAR plays beautiful piano melodies.   PanoramaLounge

🎵 Music for Dancing This Evening 🎵

6:30-7:30	The Waring Brothers play for your early evening enjoyment.	Penthouse Lounge
6:45-7:45	Ray & Shelby play your favorites.	Ports of Call, Deck 7
8:45pm	The Ship's orchestra play a pre-show set.	Palm Lounge
10-1am	Dancing music from the Waring Brothers.	Penthouse Lounge
10-11pm	Dance to your favorite melodies from Ray & Shelby.	Ports of Call, Deck 7
11:15pm	A place for nightowls! The music continues . . .	Ports of Call

---

10:30pm-11:00pm   Casino, Deck 7

CASINO CHAMPAGNE PARTY
Casino Manager and her friendly staff
invite you for a night of Casino Action!
Complimentary Champagne for all players.

Another plus you will enjoy about a cruise as opposed to a land-based vacation even at the finest hotels, is that on *any* cruise ship, the crew is always polite. They are carefully selected and trained to spoil and pamper you from the time you set foot on board until

the moment you leave. Regardless of the cruise line you choose, you *will*, with utmost certainty, receive more courteous and gracious service than you will on land.
Each of the larger ships have Las Vegas type

shows, music from disco to big band to easy listening, a casino, sauna, indoor and outdoor swimming pool(s), a movie theater showing the latest movies, and guest lecturers on a variety of subjects. If you like something in particular, you are just a few minutes away.

For single ladies, and other female passengers, who love to dance, most upscale cruise lines have "host" programs. These hosts

dance, dine play cards, and accompany you on shore excursions.

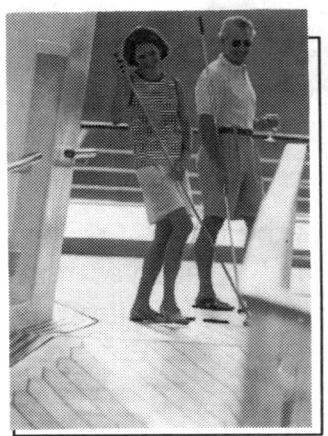

There are exercise facilities, aerobic classes, dance classes, bingo, ping pong, golf, shuffle board, swimming, skeet shooting, shopping—everything to make your cruise a perfect vacation.

Exciting, huh? These ships visit such a variety of ports, you have to see which interest you most, then choose.

Before you arrive at these destinations someone on the ship, either the Cruise Director or another expert on that particular port, will tell you about the various sights to see, where to

TUNISIA/SPAIN/FRANCE ~ 7 NIGHTS
CostaRomantica

DAY	PORT	ARRIVE	DEPART
SUN.	GENOA, ITALY		5:00 PM
MON.	NAPLES, ITALY	1:00 PM	7:00 PM
TUE.	PALERMO, SICILY	8:00 AM	7:00 PM
WED.	TUNIS, TUNISIA	7:00 AM	1:00 PM
THU.	PALMA DE MALLORCA, SPAIN	2:00 PM	MIDNIGHT
FRI.	BARCELONA, SPAIN	9:00 AM	7:00 PM
SAT.	MARSEILLE, FRANCE	8:00 AM	7:00 PM
SUN.	GENOA, ITALY	10:00 AM	

1996 SAILING DATES: 5/12, 5/19, 5/26, 6/2, 6/9, 6/16, 6/23, 6/30, 7/7, 7/14, 7/21, 7/28, 8/4, 8/11, 8/18, 8/25, 9/1, 9/8, 9/15, 9/22, 9/29, 10/6, 10/13, 10/20, 10/27

BALTIC & RUSSIA ~ 10 NIGHTS ~ AUGUST 21, 1996
CostaAllegra

DAY	PORT	ARRIVE	DEPART
AUG. 21	AMSTERDAM, NETHERLANDS		4:00 PM
AUG. 22	KIEL CANAL, GERMANY (CRUISING)	9:00 AM	5:00 PM
AUG. 23	GDYNIA, POLAND	10:00 AM	4:00 PM
AUG. 24	TALLINN, ESTONIA	2:00 PM	7:00 PM
AUG. 25	ST. PETERSBURG, RUSSIA	8:00 AM	MIDNIGHT
AUG. 26	HELSINKI, FINLAND	NOON	6:00 PM
AUG. 27	STOCKHOLM, SWEDEN	8:00 AM	6:00 PM
AUG. 28	AT SEA	-	-
AUG. 29	COPENHAGEN, DENMARK	7:00 AM	1:00 AM
AUG. 30	AT SEA	-	-
AUG. 31	AMSTERDAM, NETHERLANDS	8:00 AM	

shop, where the deals are and what to avoid. A smart thing to do when you decide on a particular trip and know the ports you'll be visiting, is to go to your bookstore and read up on these places. You can also get free information from many of the consulates. Just call them and they will mail color brochures, maps and information on tourist attractions and seasonal events.

As far as convenience, the cruise lines set up *tour*

excursions. You might have from two days to as short as several hours in some of these cities but it is truly wonderful being able to see so much in such a short time.

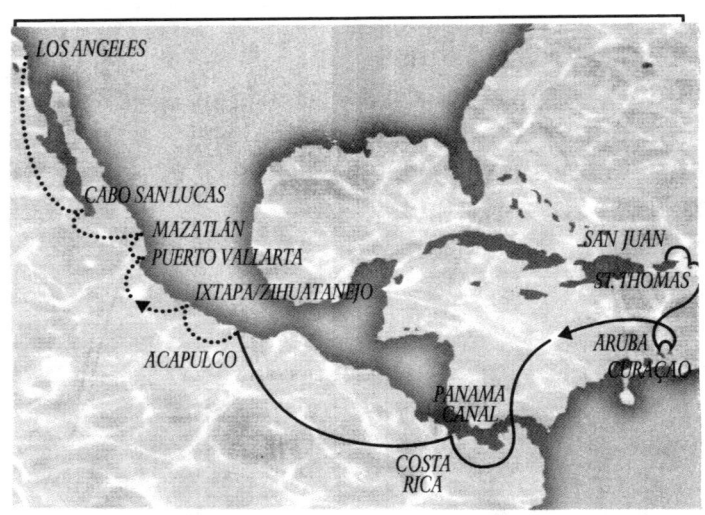

11-NIGHT SPECIAL SAILING
SAN JUAN TO ACAPULCO

SONG OF AMERICA
NOV 6/96

DAY	PORTS OF CALL	ARRIVE	DEPART
WED	SAN JUAN, PUERTO RICO		10:00 PM
THU	ST. THOMAS, USVI	8:00 AM	6:00 PM
FRI	AT SEA		
SAT	ORANJESTAD, ARUBA	8:00 AM	1:00 AM
			(SUN)
SUN	WILLEMSTAD, CURAÇAO	7:00 AM	3:00 PM
MON	AT SEA		
TUE	PANAMA CANAL (PASSAGE)	6:00 AM	5:00 PM
WED	AT SEA		
THU	CALDERA, COSTA RICA	7:00 AM	7:00 PM
FRI	AT SEA		
SAT	AT SEA		
SUN	ACAPULCO, MEXICO	8:00 AM	

7-NIGHT MEXICAN RIVIERA
ACAPULCO TO LOS ANGELES

SONG OF AMERICA
NOV 17/96

DAY	PORTS OF CALL	ARRIVE	DEPART
SUN	ACAPULCO, MEXICO		EMBARK
MON	ACAPULCO, MEXICO		6:00 PM
TUE	IXTAPA/ZIHUATANEJO, MEXICO	7:00 AM	2:00 PM
WED	PUERTO VALLARTA, MEXICO	9:00 AM	6:00 PM
THU	MAZATLÁN, MEXICO	8:00 AM	5:00 PM
FRI	CABO SAN LUCAS, MEXICO	7:00 AM	NOON
SAT	AT SEA		
SUN	LOS ANGELES, CA	10:00 AM	

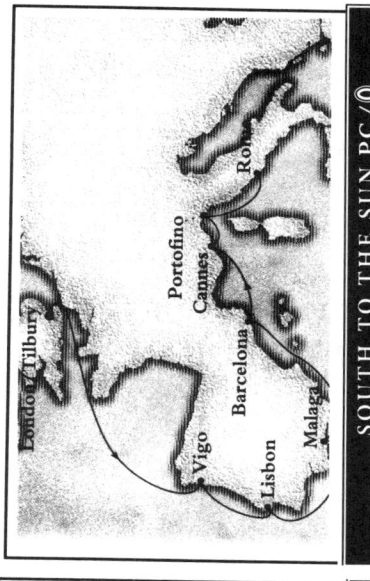

ORIENTAL CROSSROAD

Hong Kong to Bangkok (Laem Chabang) Departs October 18, 1996

Cruise 6128		Crystal Harmony	11 Days	
Date	Day	Port	Arrive	Depart
Oct 18	Fri	HONG KONG*		3 PM
Oct 19	Sat	HONG KONG		6 PM
Oct 20	Sun	Cruising the South China Sea		
Oct 21	Mon	DA NANG, VIETNAM	8 AM	6 PM
Oct 22	Tue	Cruising the South China Sea		
Oct 23	Wed	HO CHI MINH CITY, VIETNAM*	12 N	
Oct 24	Thu	HO CHI MINH CITY, VIETNAM		3 PM
Oct 25	Fri	Cruising the South China Sea		
Oct 26	Sat	SINGAPORE	8 AM	6 PM
Oct 27	Sun	KUANTAN, MALAYSIA	8 AM	5 PM
Oct 28	Mon	Cruising the Gulf of Thailand		
Oct 29	Tue	BANGKOK (LAEM CHABANG), THAILAND**	7 AM	

SOUTH TO THE SUN P.C./◎

London (Tilbury) to Rome (Civitavecchia) Departs July 24, 1996

Cruise 6216		Crystal Symphony	12 Days	
Date	Day	Port	Arrive	Depart
Jul 24	Wed	LONDON (TILBURY), ENGLAND		6 PM
Jul 25	Thu	Cruising the English Channel		
Jul 26	Fri	Cruising the Bay of Biscay		
Jul 27	Sat	VIGO, SPAIN	8 AM	6 PM
Jul 28	Sun	LISBON, PORTUGAL	8 AM	6 PM
Jul 29	Mon	GIBRALTAR, UNITED KINGDOM	1 PM	6 PM
Jul 30	Tue	MÁLAGA, SPAIN	8 AM	11 PM
Jul 31	Wed	Cruising the Mediterranean Sea		
Aug 1	Thu	BARCELONA, SPAIN	8 AM	6 PM
Aug 2	Fri	CANNES, FRANCE*	10 AM	
Aug 3	Sat	CANNES, FRANCE		5 PM
Aug 4	Sun	PORTOFINO, ITALY	8 AM	1 PM
Aug 5	Mon	ROME (CIVITAVECCHIA), ITALY	7 AM	

On the following page is a sample of a shore excursion:

FROM THE SHORE EXCURSION DESK
"A VISIT TO PETRODVORETS"

Duration: 4 Hours
Cost Per Person: $50.00

Your excursion begins with a 22-mile drive west of St. Petersburg through the suburbs to Petrodvorets. Built by Peter the Great to rival Versailles, this complex of palaces, fountains and parks is situated on the southern shore of the Gulf of Finland.

You will tour the stunning park and gardens with their incomparable network of mountains that cascade through the picture-perfect setting. The gilded fountains use close to 7,500 gallons of water per minute. The centerpiece is a statue of Samson rending the jaw of a lion, prominently placed in front of the Grand Palace. The elaborate system of fountains has been restored after virtual destruction during WWII. Inside the palace, the State Apartments are sumptuously appointed, especially the Partridge Drawing Room with brilliantly refurbished silk-covered walls adorned with the birds which give the room it's name. Although it may no longer be the original "Peterhof" created in the 18th century, Petrodvorets could not have been more painstakingly restored.

Note: This excursion involves substantial walking.

The deadline for ordering the above tour is 11:30am on Tuesday, 1st of August. Please use your Booking Form and place in the box at the Shore Excursion Desk, Deck 6.

PRE-SAIL AND POST-SAIL PROGRAMS

There are also pre-sail and post-sail programs that are being offered by many cruise lines, depending on your destination. Ask your travel agent to get this information for you. It just means to schedule your air transportation to arrive days (or weeks) earlier, or leave days or weeks after your cruise.

For instance, let's say you want to take a cruise that goes to some exciting cities in Europe. Chances are your port of embarkation is London. So, fly to London before (or stay after) your cruise.

Many cruise lines charge approximately $35 to $50 per person for what they term an "air deviation" which will bring you in early or keep you a day or so later. If you take the cruise lines pre- or post-cruise tour packages, they do all the transfers and they usually have great *deals!* Check with your travel agent.

For adventure, you could schedule a trip on the famous *Orient Express,* which travels from London to Paris, Zurich, Innsbruck and Venice, and then begin your cruise.

Perhaps after you take a cruise to the Orient, you just aren't ready to return home. Well, the *Eastern and Oriental Express* runs between Bangkok and Singapore. Visit any number of adventurous, unusual or just relaxing cities you'd like to see before your vacation is over.

EVERYTHING on a cruise is done for you. If you want to  just "turn yourself over to them" you will get the vacation of a lifetime! You simply have to enjoy yourself. The staff will do their best to make it a memorable vacation.

Remember, eight, ten or twelve cities to visit on a two-week cruise vacation, yet you pack and unpack but one time!

As you read through this book, we will attempt to cover almost everything you'll encounter on a cruise. In our combined 50 years of cruising, we've seen it all—and we've survived.

Cruising is the only way to go!

Chapter 2

YOUR FIRST CRUISE

The smartest move, we advise, is to read this entire book, select a date and destination to cruise, then go to a nearby travel agency and pick up an armload of cruise brochures to take home and read.

These brochures and ship itineraries might tend to confuse you, so you and your traveling companion (if you're not traveling alone) have to make your decision about where to cruise? You already know the date and length of time you have, whether you'll take the kids along or "store" them with a friend or relative. Now comes the task of reading these enticing glossy brochures that do their utmost to "sell" you on their particular cruise line. Here are some things to consider.

COST

If price is the key factor, find the ships that offer the price you can afford and then begin the choosing process. In the chapter about cruise ships we tell you the prices available as of this writing. Remember, there are also early-booking and various other discounts that could be available. Don't forget, ask your travel agent about the current discounts, happenings and specials.

To give you the cost of these various cruises is difficult. Besides, we'd like you to read our entire book and find out about all the cruise lines and their ships.

A "ballpark figure" for a cruise to the Caribbean for 7 days is a low as $100 a day and as much as—well as much as you'd like to pay. We tell you about all the ships, the expensive ones and the deals.

Since most of the cruise ships go to the same areas of the world, once you have a price, look for the ports you are most interested in visiting. If you choose a Mediterranean cruise, for example, look for the cities you would most like to visit and toss aside the brochures that do not include these cities.

Then again, if price is all-important, you might have to choose a *few* ports that aren't your favorites to make the ports you like—with the price you can afford! Don't be shy about asking for a "deal." Travel agents are human and most of them live on a budget too.

CHOOSING A CABIN

These photos are of cabins aboard Norwegian Cruise Line's ship, *Leeward.* A large factor in cost is the type of cabin

Inside Stateroom

you choose. When reading the itinerary of a cruise line that also includes prices, you can readily see that the

Deluxe Outside Stateroom

Superior Deluxe Outside Stateroom

least desirable cabin costs the least. First time cruisers, choose the cabin you can afford. There are inside cabins which mean no widows. Who cares? You eat the same food, enjoy the same entertainment, and visit the same ports of call regardless of the cabin you have.

As you move up the price ladder, the cabins get roomier, have larger windows, double beds, bathtub and shower, etc.

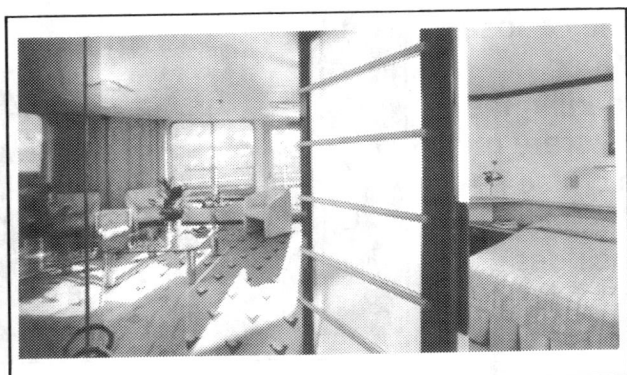

Superior Deluxe Penthouse with Private Balcony

This chart from Crystal Cruises will show the difference in cabin prices.

Categories		Cruise Fares	Group Fares	Special Single Fares
CP	Crystal Penthouse w/verandah	$21,170	N/A	N/A
PS	Penthouse Suite w/verandah	14,480	$11,584	$17,376
PH	Penthouse w/verandah	11,540	9,232	13,848
A	Deluxe Stateroom w/verandah	8,230	6,173	7,099
B	Deluxe Stateroom w/verandah	7,910	5,933	6,823
C	Deluxe Stateroom	7,285	5,464	6,284
D	Deluxe Stateroom	6,995	5,246	6,033
E	Deluxe Stateroom w/part. view	6,730	5,048	5,805

SIZE OF SHIPS

You might also want to choose a *size* ship that you feel most comfortable with. Ships are measured (not weighed) in gross registered tons (grt) and carry from 100 passengers to approximately 2,500 passengers. Look not only for the **tonnage** of a ship but also look at how many **passengers** it carries and then decide on what you feel most comfortable with. No matter which ship you choose, they *all* offer a place to sleep, food to eat, they travel to various ports, and furnish entertainment and service.

SEASICKNESS

Forget it! Your chances of being seasick are from slim to none on these giant ships. Many people who have gone offshore fishing in small boats have felt as if they would like to be tossed overboard and end it all then and there. But on today's cruise ships, this is how it works.

These vessels travel only the calmest waters in the world. And, with the stabilizers on these modern ships and advance weather reports, you can hardly feel the ship move at all! If you are *really* susceptible to motion sickness, talk to your physician before the cruise for their recommendation. If you are *sorta* vulnerable to motion sickness, get some of these innovative "patches" or "wristbands" before you leave on your trip from your local pharmacy.

Should you forget to take these precautions and you begin to feel queasy while aboard the ship, take a trip to the ship's doctor for a handful of free pills or see what they have to offer as far as medication.

WHAT MONEY TO CARRY

Since almost everything is included in your fare, and what isn't can be signed for, there's no need to carry your wallet with you aboard most ships, except to show other passengers pictures of your kids.

Most ships *do not* include liquor in their quoted cruise-fare price, and if you want a haircut, massage, whatever—you just sign and pay your bill at the end of the cruise by cash, travelers check or credit card. (Some cruise lines will not take a personal check.).

THINGS TO ASK YOUR TRAVEL AGENT

The tired *cliche*, "An once of prevention is worth a pound of cure" fits right here. We don't want to make this "dream vacation" seem like work but there is a certain amount of information you need to know before you leave or it just might dampen your fun time. It's far better to know what to expect now than to have it "sprung" on you when you're thousands of miles away and at sea.

✔Ask about "hidden costs"—because cruise lines differ in what they offer. Additional costs might include this particular ship's tipping policy, port taxes, the price of drinks, medical attention, visas (to visit Russia, etc.), and babysitting costs if you're *dragging* young children along.

✔Ask if the cruise line offers **early-booking discounts** or other incentives. If you book early, you not only get a choice of the best cabins but also the best price. And make certain you are **guaranteed** to receive any price reductions on the cruise prior to sailing.

✔Ask what their **cancellation policy** is in the event there is a mishap in your life before the cruise. (Usually you get a full refund up to 60 days prior to sailing.) We've listed information on insurance in this chapter.

✔Ask if your travel agent has errors and omissions insurance, and if so, by whom? Deal *only* with travel agents who are reputable and well recommended.

✔Ask if there will be children on board. If you hate kids (or are taking your own) you should know if this particular cruise caters to families or if it's mostly adults. Your brochures should tell you but ask your travel agent anyway. If your cabin is large enough and occupied by two full-fare paying passengers, children (or any third or fourth passenger) sail at a much reduced rate.

✔Ask if the air fare is included in the cruise price, and if so, ask from where to where? This is a great savings since cruise lines get deals and air discounts that they can pass on to you. (If, however, you live a hundred or so miles from a major city, chances are high that they will not land in your tiny airport.)

✔Ask your travel agent the ratio of the crew to the number of passengers. From 40% to 50% crew-to-passenger ratio is ideal, this means you have a better chance of getting fast service.

✔Also, ask what the passenger-to-space ratio is. A 40+ the best, 30+ and above is usually ideal; between 20-30 is still livable without getting *squished*, and between 10-20 is rather high density. Below 10, you're on a cattle boat.

✔Ask your travel agent if they have *personally* been on a cruise. We think it's important that they have, because anybody can read and look at photos and at video tapes but to *feel* and experience a cruise is the only way to tell others about it. In addition, ask if they've sailed with this particular cruise line, perhaps this very ship. They will be able to tell you *exactly* what to expect.

✔Ask any question, regardless how stupid it might seem. Better to ask **now!**

INSURANCE

First, let's assume that you and your spouse are about to take a cruise you've planned and saved for. And, a week *before* the cruise, you, your traveling companion or someone dear to you has an auto accident or gets extremely ill, what do you do?

Suppose you're already *on* a cruise and you break a leg or become ill in a foreign country, who pays for what?

The last thing we want to do is to frighten you or to act like *profits of doom* but to be realistic, the *only* way to avoid such a mishap is to insure against it! We realize you might be on a budget, but our advice is to save but a bit longer and get insurance. Here are some questions to ask which may help you decide.

❶ Would all my vacation money be refunded if I canceled my trip because of an accident or medical problems? Would this include my traveling companion, parents or children?

❷ Could I handle a medical, legal, or a similar emergency in a non-English speaking country? At night? During the weekend? On a holiday?

❸ If hospitalized abroad, could I arrange for the required payment in advance for medical treatment? Many foreign hospitals withhold your passport until they receive full payment.

❹ Would there be an additional cost to fly home before the end of my trip if I or a member of my family back home became seriously ill? Would the cost of the remainder of my trip be refunded?

There is **full cancellation insurance** in the event you must miss the trip for any reason. Without this insurance, if you cancel at the last minute, you could lose every cent you paid. The estimated cost of this insurance depends on the price and length of the cruise. For example, a 7-day cruise is approximately $90-$135; a 14-day cruise, $120-$170 per person.

There is new insurance being offered that covers pre-existing illnesses. These policies must be purchased at the time of the cruise deposit. For instance, if you have a record of heart trouble or chronic illness, regular insurance might not cover it. Better to ask!

PHYSICALLY CHALLENGED

If you have a physical disability and must use a wheelchair, it's best to book early. Most of the luxury ships have these special cabins but not many. Make certain they have large enough doors to fit a wheelchair through.

CUSTOMIZE YOUR CRUISE

Your travel agent will customize your cruise for you. These giant luxury ships travel just about every place in the world with different cruise itineraries, length of trips and whenever you plan to or would like to cruise, it's there for you. If your travel agent can determine exactly what you want (and can afford) they will, without a doubt, match you with your perfect cruise.

PASSPORTS

Going to a foreign country? Passport offices are located in Federal Buildings in all large cities. Or, go to your local post office, fill out a form and send it in. Instructions are included. It normally takes six weeks by mail. You can pay extra and speed up the process if you need the passport in a week or so. The cost of a passport (good for 10 years) is $55.

You will need two passport photos. Most malls have a location to take these photos. No need to get a glamour shot; these checkers look only for a reasonable likeness. Just don't show it around if you don't like the photo.

PACKING

Once you select a ship, date, and itinerary, you'll

have an *idea* of the type of clothes to pack. Most first-time cruise passengers take far too much. Airlines allow you two suitcases each with a total weight of 70 pounds. More, and you (usually) pay extra. You are also allowed one carry-on piece of luggage. Use this for books, aspirin, antacid tablets, maybe your better jewelry, reading glasses, sunglasses, pamphlets on tours, etc.

Several weeks in advance, of your departure date, the cruise line will send you a large packet of information with a list of tours and a detailed list of the special nights and events to help you choose the appropriate clothing. Just about all cruise ships accept casual dress during the day and on tours. Enjoy yourself. Be comfortable.

For evening meals there are (usually) early and late seating, like 6 or 8pm. Check the Daily Itinerary to help you decide what to wear that evening. Many ships require coat and tie—their brochure will tell you. On formal nights men wear a tuxedo or a dark suit, and ladies an evening dress. Shirley and I like dressing for dinner. These exquisite dinners taste even better if you're dressed to the hilt.

It's really an experience, like living in your own castle. You dress in your room, lock your cabin, and stroll mere minutes to a lavish dining room with tables of passengers, all with smiling faces and dressed in their finery. It's like a dream.

Occasionally, after a busy day, you may prefer room service. The menus are extensive and the service prompt.

PACKING FOR MEN

You're going to have to decide for yourself how many pairs of socks and shorts and T-shirts to bring. If you have a runny nose, don't forget those handkerchiefs. Then, there's cufflinks, buttons for the tux shirt, walking shorts, belt(s) and maybe suspenders.

For men on a 10-day cruise, there are as many as four evenings where formal attire is suggested. Pete recommends one dark suit or tuxedo, a few different styles (or colored) shirts and several ties. It makes it look like a different outfit. Dark shoes are okay; patent leather is for the *Oscar* awards, weddings, and the QE-2, *Grill Class*.

Maybe throw in a sports jacket and a few pairs of pants, and take along a blue blazer and white pants, sort of a nautical, yachtsman look, you know.

For the day and some evening

meals, strictly casual. Two or three pairs of Dockers and four or five shirts with collars. Loafers or deck shoes are accepted. Bring your most comfortable (new not recommended) walking shoes and a few jogging suits for tours. Over the years we've converted the world to jogging suits and Reeboks. Nobody cares, just be comfortable.

Don't forget swim trunks, and maybe a "fanny pouch" (butt bag) for wearing on tours. A neat item to wear is a vest (sort of like a hunting vest) with *mucho* pockets to keep a camera, binoculars, small souvenirs, extra film, ship's lunch, etc. Buy one a size larger to fit over a shirt or jacket.

Finally, bring your toiletries, credit cards, some cash, traveler checks and yourself. And don't forget pictures of your kids. Others at the table will just *love* that! Take along two large suitcases (even if you pack each half-full) to bring home souvenirs.

And, Oh! Type out a list from your bulky address book or Rolodex of everyone you plan to send a postcard to. As you send one, scratch their name from the list. The ship will have postcards but it's usually more fun to shop for them at your different ports of call. It's easier to get stamps on the ship. Just sign a voucher and pay for them at the end of your cruise and have them mail your correspondence. For many countries, you'll be home before your cards or letters.

PACKING FOR WOMEN

Shirley recommends dark, cocktail-length dresses for the evening and at least one evening gown, or choose what you feel most comfortable (or look) best in. Glitter and glamour is in for dinner. Beaded tops and a sparkling jacket will dress up anything in your wardrobe. Scarves, jewelry and an upswept hairstyle can change the look of a basic dress if you find you need to wear it twice. Also, a light wrap may be necessary for a stroll along the deck.

The ship's boutique is stocked with beaded bags, belts and all the extras you may need or forgot to include. Her suggestion is to bring as many clothes as you are allowed. If you don't wear something, so what? But if you don't *have* something, it's not a disaster. Just splurge and make that much-needed purchase at the boutique. After all, it *is* a vacation.

Something smart to pack in your luggage is a small canvas or nylon bag for carrying snacks on tours, camera, souvenirs, and for sample-size toiletries. If you forget it, you can always find others to buy with names of the different countries embroidered or stamped on them.

This same extra bag can accommodate a book, stationery, change of shoes, or whatever for the poolside on the at-sea days. And, there is never enough room in your luggage for your purchases on the return trip home. This extra bag will again come in handy. And so will a small container of *Woolite* for washing lingerie or underwear in your room. And for the end of your voyage, maybe pack two large garbage bags for dirty clothes. They have plastic bags in the cabins but they are far too small.

AIRPORT TO DESTINATION

For your flight, check your luggage in at the airport the same as if you're traveling on any airplane flight. The only exception is your pre-flight package from the cruise line will contain luggage tags with your ship's name. Print your name and address on those tags along with your preassigned cabin number and fasten onto each piece of your luggage.

When you arrive at your destination, retrieve your luggage as you ordinarily do and look for the cruise line representative who will be carrying a large sign that is stapled to a long stick with the name of your cruise line. They will direct you to the special check-in counters, marked in large letters with the first letter of your surname, to help you pass through customs easily.

We favor the Air-Sea packages, not only because they save you money, but because when you arrive at your destination at a huge airport that is unfamiliar, it is possible to wander indefinitely. If you have this package, you can count on their representative being there.

After this check-in business is over, your ship's representative will tell you where to stack your luggage and then—*just forget it.* The next time you see your bags, they will be aboard the ship in your cabin.

The person with the sign will then direct you to your group's transportation. They are usually independent transport companies not associated with the cruise line. If the shuttle ride is an hour or more, it's nice to tip the driver of the bus. Use your own discretion.

Also, depending upon the time of your arrival, and length of your flight, most of the time, the cruise line includes an overnight stay at a "good" hotel, along with arrangements to take you to the ship the following morning. (This is not available to those who don't have the air/sea package.)

BOARDING YOUR SHIP

When you arrive at your ship, you will proceed up the gangway and come face to face (for the first of many times) with a photographer to take your picture. Do it! They are not free, but you can look at them in a day or two after they're developed and then decide whether or not to purchase.

As you step on board, you'll meet the ships greeting staff, receive your boarding pass and be shown to your cabin by a steward who will magically appear to help you with hand luggage. No tip required.

Look over your cabin while the steward is there to see if everything is as was represented to you. If not, tell the steward **immediately** and he will assist you. Chances are your cabin will be spotless, but "turnaround" time on some ships is mere hours. If you find a lost possession from a previous tenant, turn it in to your cabin steward.

There will be a *shipboard* packet of information in your cabin. Be certain to read it right away. In it is a list of activities for that evening and a ship directory (map) giving you the layout of the ship and a lot of information you'll need to know. If you're on a very large ship, you may feel more comfortable carrying the map in your pocket for a few days to find your way to the dining room, casino, sauna and back to your cabin, etc.

SAFETY DRILL

Each ship will conduct a Safety/Lifeboat Drill within 24 hours of sailing. You will be instructed by the ship's intercom as to where your life preserver is, how to put it on properly, and be advised where to go with it. These lifeboat stations are assigned by deck and posted on the back of each cabin door. Not only is the lifeboat drill required participation but it's also a splendid time to meet some of the other passengers.

You'll be given routine "abandon ship/lifeboat" instructions, and then, the captain and crew will pass by and smile, greet you, and maybe shake your hand. It's fun! (Don't forget your camera, and take a picture with your life vest on.)

Everything about taking a cruise is fun! As often as we've both traveled, the adrenalin begins to pump the closer we get to making that drive from our home to the airport to begin yet another cruise.

First time cruisers, you'll love it!

Chapter 3

HOW TO REALLY ENJOY YOUR CRUISE

To you first-time cruise passengers, your first cruise is a once-in-a-lifetime dream; a vacation you've saved for and planned, possibly for a long time. There are a few things, however, that will dampen your cruise and here is one of them. Our suggestion is to avoid . . .

WHINGERS

On a recent cruise to Germany, Russia and the Scandinavian countries, during the bus ride from Tilbury to Gatwick Airport in London where we were to catch our flight back to the US, the personable and experienced London guide on the bus spoke of a "whinger." He said it was a new word used in the travel guide business. We couldn't find it in the dictionary, but it should be. It's become a part of our personal vocabulary since.

A *whinger* (**win-je´r**) or to *whinge,* means to complain, demand, gripe, nag, be negative, and make life miserable for everyone around you. Woefully, whingers are everywhere! And our message to you is to stay as far away from them as possible. Regardless of what you say to them, know that you're not going to change them; they are either born that way or have practiced being miserable until it has become a part of their daily routine. Just smile and move away.

ALL AGES ABOARD

On these cruises, you'll discover that (usually) the *longer* the cruise, the *older* the people. This is mainly because we "older folk" who have worked all our lives, can afford a cruise that costs five or six thousand dollars or more. The "younger folk" take those 3 to 7-day jaunts that cost substantially less and party constantly.

The word "old" is such a relative term. We've all seen "old" people who were 25 and "young" people at 85. You have too, haven't you? Never judge a person's health, vigor, attitude or sex-drive, chronologically.

ATTITUDE

Regardless of your age, your attitude is of utmost importance, especially when traveling to far-off lands with 99% strangers surrounding you. We say, don't keep them as strangers. Chances are (other than the whingers) they are all nice people. Smile, be friendly and talk to them.

CHECKLIST TO HELP YOU ENJOY YOUR CRUISE

✔We're hoping you asked your travel agent everything you'd like to know and that you are satisfied and insured.

✔Remember, pack as much as you feel comfortable with. And bring along a camera and plenty of film (less expensive at home than onboard or overseas). If you bought a new camera, test it *before* the cruise.

✔Leave some money in a secret place in your locked automobile to pay the parking in the event the ship's casino sends you home rather "light." And maybe some additional money to get fresh milk and bread for breakfast.

✔We suggest you make sure battery cables are in your trunk just in case your car battery goes down. There are emergency services at parking facilities but there is a fee to give you a jump start. Better yet, have a family member take you to and pick you up at the airport and leave your car at home. Less trouble when boarding to be dropped off at the airport entrance.

✔Travel with, or be around, people you enjoy. Don't allow anyone to mess up your glorious vacation.

✔Don't forget to bring small bills ($1's, $5's and $10's) for tipping and buying junk souvenirs. AND—bring those credit cards.

CREDIT CARDS

Speaking of credit cards, remember to jot down your card number, and a worldwide 800# in case of loss or theft. This information should be kept with your luggage, not in your purse or wallet. Should an unfortunate incident occur you will be able to report your card and be issued a new one which shouldn't inconvenience your shopping more than a day or two. We suggest bringing two credit cards *each* in the event you lose or misplace one, your traveling companion has a duplicate. And the second one in the event the "well runs dry" on your first one.

✔You might be in three countries with different currency in three days. By the time you have one currency down pat, a new one is waiting for you at the next port. A very handy device is a currency converter, a paper no larger than a cassette. It automatically converts US dollars to whatever currency you need. It's much easier than trying to figure if a purchase is a bargain in the heat of the negotiating process. "Let's see if one dollar equals $1,200 Lira, then $13,000 Lira means *this really costs* about . . ." Get this currency converter at your local book store.

✔Should family members need to contact you, leave a copy of your itinerary with them. Also, keep your ship's schedule in your fanny pack during shore leaves. Should you become separated from your group and need to meet with the ship in the next port you will have that information. *It's happened more than once.*

✔Lots of seasoned travelers bring their long distance calling card to make easy, direct, phone calls to family and friends to remind them how much fun they are having!

✔Visas—not required in most countries but are required in Russia, Brazil and Australia. Your travel agent can recommend a service but, usually, the cruise line will make the necessary arrangements for the entire ship by obtaining a master visa.

TRAVELERS CHECKS

It almost seems unnecessary to convert large sums of cash into traveler's checks. We think the credit card has eliminated the need of travelers checks no matter what Karl Malden says. Our standard procedure is to take several hundred dollars in American currency with us, a few hundred in travelers checks, and those *two* different credit cards (in the event we exceed our limit.)

As far as safety against getting robbed or losing our money, we would go from the airport in the USA to our airport in, let's say London or Paris. Immediately the cruise representative would usher us onto the bus and transport us either to a hotel or directly to the ship. Upon reaching our cabin, we would lock our cash and credit cards in the drawer or in the ship's vault. Not much chance of getting robbed during this time.

CONVERTING CURRENCY

On board the ship, prior to disembarking in a country, we would use our traveler's checks or cash to convert to the local currency. We would leave one credit card in our locked drawer and take the other ashore with us for purchases in the better stores or shops. We would also have that wad of $1's and $5's for tipping or for postcards or small souvenir purchases and maybe *some* extra cash.

We have found that most countries accept US currency readily. And, to our surprise, the dollar had a strong purchasing power. The "big" stores take credit cards or travelers checks. The street merchants usually take local currency (maybe US dollars). If you happen to decide you absolutely cannot *live* without that set of camel bells or a statue of Zeus, or two dozen T-shirts, you'll find a way to make the buy.

If you do get travelers checks, get the kind that both you *and* your traveling companion can cash in case one of you is not available for a signature. And yes, make note of the series of numbers, again in your luggage, in case they are lost or stolen.

CHOOSING COMPANIONS

Assuming you're not traveling in a group or with friends, most first-time cruise passengers will seek out a person or couple to serve as traveling companions. We've done it on just about every cruise. We like people!

First, you have part of a day, an evening and maybe another full day aboard the ship to meet people and get acquainted before you reach your first port. You'll be with them at dinner, stand next to them during your lifeboat drill or perhaps on the bus ride from the airport to the ship. Be ready to choose. It isn't easy to tell *all* about a person or couple in this short time but you will get somewhat of an idea of their personality, what they like and how they will act.

On one cruise we saw a couple at the airport who seemed to enjoy being with each other. For any number of reasons, they sort of "stuck out" from all the others. They were about the right age, they smiled, had some problem with their tickets but didn't complain and we said *hello* with our eyes. Sure enough, we met them on board our ship and we became constant traveling companions.

On another cruise, we heard a group of 3 couples laughing and having a great time aboard the bus from the airport to the ship. One couple in particular seemed compatible. We "hooked up" with them for the entire cruise and had a wonderful time.

Yet another time we sort of "bumped into" a couple as we were going down the gangplank who looked fun and we decided to share our shore excursions with them. It didn't work. It won't always work. That evening while looking in the window at the gift shop we met another couple—and they were fun.

However, choosing shore excursion partners is almost like a blind date; who knows if it will pan out? But, in not *too* much time you'll know and you can easily "get lost" or drift away without a problem. There's no need to mess up a fun time with a person or couple you'll probably never see again.

PROBLEMS YOU CAN'T DO ANYTHING ABOUT

On just about every ship, there are a multitude of things that can happen; its *Murphy's Law.* But, these cruise lines are aware of all of these potential problems; nothing's new. They strive arduously to make your cruise as delightful as God permits. With anywhere from 300 to over 4,000 (passengers and crew) on one ship there will be problems. Just don't let it detract from or erase what should be a remarkable vacation.

On a recent cruise about 60 of us were on a bus that took us from the port at Warnamunde to Berlin. I'd liked to have cruised there, but Berlin wasn't that coopera-tive; it's still a hundred or so miles from the water. The bus ride was to be three hours long. Hey, how bad could it be? The answer, pretty bad.

The tour bus advertised *air conditioning* written in English. But there is a difference between what *we* call air conditioning and what *they* call air conditioning. Their idea of air conditioning was to turn on something that made a noise and had a motor. Perhaps it wasn't working that day, even though it was a Mercedes Benz.

When we made our first stop I looked on the roof and the so called "air conditioning" was some *air scoops* that literally allowed the hot air in as the bus motored down the highway. The outside temperature was perhaps 90° so we were "air conditioned" by hot, 90° air being blown at us by what seemed like a dozen or so thirsty hounds breathing their dog breath on us. These things happen. By the time we returned to the ship (after a half hour delay while they fixed a flat) it was a contest as to which bus was the worst. Sadly, we won. But it's all part of the adventure or traveling.

CAN'T GO TO EGYPT

A few years ago on a cruise whose destination was primarily the Greek Isles, we were supposed to visit Egypt and—they canceled. Why? Because it was unsafe at that time! Many passengers were disappointed because of not being able to see the pyramids or to ride a camel. The cruise line had no other option than to schedule an alternate port. So, we spent an extra day some place else and got to ride a camel in Jerusalem.

There will be other cruises that include Egypt. And, a camel ride is not such a thrill. Camels are, basically, creatures without manners. They spit, snort, lick, bite, smell badly and the ride is neither with shocks nor air conditioning.

THERE'S A WAR GOING ON

Again, the same thing happened in Dubrovnik, Yugoslavia. We were scheduled to go there but there was a *war going on!* The cruise line selected an alternate port where we could visit and nobody was killed or wounded. The *Whingers* of course, were in full concert!

TOUR DIRECTOR or HOTEL MANAGER

If you're on a tour and have a problem, go to the person directing the tour. Your comfort (or discomfort) is their responsibility. If you're not on a tour and on the ship, go immediately to your room steward. If they can't help, go to the *Hotel Manager.*

I know it sounds strange to have a hotel manager on a cruise ship but after all, remember this ship is as large as many hotels and hotel managers on cruise ships are selected as carefully as they select the captain because they are responsible for everything other than the mechanics of running the ship.

CRUISE DIRECTORS

Gosh, what a job these Cruise Directors have. They travel everywhere free, they eat gourmet meals free, their rent is paid for, and they get paid for doing it! Let me tell you, they *deserve* whatever they get and more because—they earn it!

The Cruise Directors and their team of assistants do everything! They call the bingo games, either give or assist in the port talks, teach the dance lessons, schedule special interest talks and activities, they emcee the shows, and plan the fun itinerary on the ship. They never seem to sleep. (*Legend* among cruise directors is Fernando deOliviera, formerly with Royal Cruise Line.)

TRAVELING ALONE and/or SHARING A CABIN

There are ships that offer single cabins. Space is at a premium aboard ship and a single cabin cost a bit more than if two people were sharing the cabin. So if you want privacy, be willing to pay more for it. In recent years, more than a million people took cruises without a companion.

Most cruise lines offer a GUARANTEED SHARE program. This is where you pay the "double" room rate and the cruise line *finds* another passenger who is traveling alone, and always of the same sex and your approximate age. Be certain to specify a smoking or non-smoking roommate. As far as sharing a cabin with a stranger, that *is* an adventure.

Sometimes, the "other person" doesn't show and you will only pay for a double cabin occupancy at a reduced rate and be in the cabin alone.

ROMANCE

The television series *THE LOVE BOAT* had many seasons of fun, romantic episodes that promoted many single people to cruise for romance. The fact of the matter is, that romance between singles happens often aboard a cruise ship.

Most people who cruise are educated, financially stable and enjoy fun. When you put two fun people together in an atmosphere of luxury, music, entertainment, travel, adventure and all the ambiance of a cruise ship, romance is a distinct possibility.

Being consenting adults, the cruise line cares not who goes with whom. The maitre D' will try to seat singles at a table with other singles. There are cocktail parties, meals and many events tailored especially for singles.

SEX ON CRUISE SHIPS

Cruise lines are always concerned about *customer satisfaction* but, up until now, that meant the guests should find the soup hot, the cabin temperature to their liking and making sure the servers were friendly and efficient.

Royal Caribbean Cruise Line, however, has gone behind the closed cabin doors to check out passenger satisfaction, with a Sex at Sea poll, conducted with Cosmopolitan magazine.

After interviewing 2,000 passengers, the survey found 95% of respondents rated cruises as "extremely or very romantic" compared with a land-based vacation.

Nearly half—48%—said they had sex as many as six times a week on their cruise vacation compared to their usual once or twice weekly at home. The survey didn't stop there. It found most passengers—79%—packed sexy lingerie or underwear, and one in three brought body lotions or massage oils on board.

Although these accessories often are thought to be the domain of women, the survey found that 73% of male passengers packed special underwear and out-numbered the women when it came to body lotions, massage oils, romantic or sex toys and novelty condoms.

When asked where on board they would have sex if given the chance, guests passionately suggested:

The Whirlpool
The Royal Suite
An elevator
A lifeboat
The Bridge

HOST PROGRAM

For whatever reason, there always seems to be a preponderance of single women on cruises. Or, married women traveling alone whose husbands are either at home watching TV with the remote control becoming a permanent part of their anatomy, or they are hunting, fishing or playing golf.

Women like to travel and most women love to dance. Recognizing this problem, many cruise lines have gone to great lengths to gather up mature single

men—who absolutely like being around people—to serve as non-paid hosts. The success of this program has been phenomenal and is now a charming and permanent fixture aboard most luxury ships.

On each cruise, these highly recommended, distinguished, congenial single gentlemen, (usually retirees) are invited aboard as "unofficial" shipboard hosts to passengers. They will dance with you, dine with you, play cards with you and act as social partners for ladies traveling alone. They accompany these ladies on shore excursions, attend cocktail parties with them and participate in other shipboard activities.

They have explicit instructions—rules if you may—that they are to show no favoritism toward any passenger or group; they are to mingle and not remain with any one partner no matter how compelling the fascination. Romantic relationships are strictly prohibited! Both the female passengers and the hosts are implored to trust that the rules are as specified. If the rules are broken, these hosts are immediately dismissed.

The cruise lines are very discriminating as to whom they select as hosts. Each is recommended to the line by a reputable travel agency or by a close friend who is already part of the program. These men are carefully screened and personally interviewed by a selected staff. While on board, they are directed and monitored by the ship's officers.

Selections are based on a combination of attributes. They must be congenial, respectable and have travel experience. They must like people, have almost boundless enthusiasm about participating in a variety of events and social activities and they are to participate in nightly dancing. It isn't necessary that they be professional dancers but most are very good because they love to dance. We've met many of them and they were all bright, delightful, and fun.

Chapter 4

LET'S HAVE FUN WITH FOOD

And last but not least, the food. We think the most talked-about item on any cruise is the cuisine. Without going into great detail, the menus on these cruises are from excellent to superb. It's mentioned on the intro-

ductory page that you can eat 12 meals or more per day but the truth is, food is available 24 hours a day!

The evening meal is a dining experience. Imagine yourself dressed in finery enjoying the company of other vacationers and in a fabulous restaurant with a menu prepared by some of the top chefs in the world.

If you don't like what the menu offers, ask your waiter for what you

want and if humanly possible, you'll get it. To use a worn cliche, *Your wish is their command!* How *much* you eat is up to you. If you want two entrees or three or several portions of one, maybe an entire meal of appetizers. Or you'd like three desserts, simply ask for them. Most first-time cruisers (even those who have taken 63 cruises), stuff themselves. We say, "Go for it!" If you're worried about a rapid weight gain, experience is that you'll lose the extra weight you put on in a matter of days after you return to your own cooking and eating routine.

The fact of the matter is, most humans rarely experience such food—unless they go on a cruise. We rate most of the food served on cruise ships from excellent to outstanding. And remember, if you don't like it, don't eat it! Order something else and tell them exactly how you want it prepared! They will attempt to please even the most discriminating.

There is no better way to *tell* you about the food served on most luxury ships other than to show you some of the menus. Below is a typical BREAKFAST MENU aboard a Carnival Cruise Line ship.

BREAKFAST EXPRESS
Orange Juice, Scrambled Eggs, Crisp Bacon, Toast and Beverage

CHILLED JUICES
Orange   Pineapple   Grapefruit   Apple   Tomato   Prune

FANCY FRUITS
Grapefruit Half   Banana   Orange and Grapefruit Sections
Melon in Season   Baked Apple   Stewed Prunes

CEREALS
(All cereals served with Regular or Skimmed Milk)

Corn Flakes   Frosted Flakes   Special K   Sugar Pops
All Bran   Raison Bran   Rice Krispies   40% Bran Flakes

Hot Cream of Wheat   Hot Oatmeal

BREAKFAST ENTREES

Eggs Carnival
Boiled, Scrambled, Fried
Poached on Toast, As You Prefer

Buttermilk Pancakes
Old Fashioned Style
Warm and Delicious

Eggs Benedict
Our Classic Preparation

French Toast
Served with Syrup or Honey

Lox 'n Bagels
Sliced Nova Scotia Salmon
Served Cold with a Toasted Bagel
Cream Cheese

Omelette Eggsceptionale
A Light, Fluffy Omelette
Prepared Plain, with Ham, and
Cheese or Combination

BREAKFAST SPECIALTY OF THE DAY
Our Chef Prepares a Different Breakfast Specialty Each Day.
Please Ask Your Server About Today's Creation
Low Cholesterol Egg Substitute Available Upon Request

ON THE SIDE
Corned Beef Hash   Sliced Breakfast Ham   Hominy Grits
Hickory Smoked Bacon Hash Browned Potatoes Breakfast Link Sausages

FROM THE BAKERY
Danish   Croissants   Muffins
Plain and Raison English Muffins, Bagels
White, Whole Wheat and Rye Toast, Served with Guava, Strawberry and
Grape Jellies. Orange Marmalade and Honey
Diet Jellies Served on Request

BEVERAGES
Freshly Brewed Coffee: Regular or Decaffeinated Tea, Milk,
Skimmed Milk or Hot Chocolate

LUNCHEON MENU

SOUPS
Chinese Eggdrop
Cream of Spinach

SALADS
Cottage Cheese, Sliced Tomatoes
Greek Salad
*Iceberg Lettuce, Cucumber, Tomatoes,
Olives and Feta Cheese in a Light Vinaigrette*

LUNCHEON ENTREES

Tropical Fruit Plate
*Wedges of Juicy Pineapple, Cantaloupe,
Apples, Pears and more. Served with a
Honey-Yogurt Dressing*

Fusillie with Seafood
*Spiral Pasta with Shrimp, Scallops, Clams
and Mussels in a Chardonnay Sauce*

Western Omelette
*A Three-Egg Fluffy Melette with Ham
Peppers and Cheese*

Roasted Turkey Sandwich
*Served Cold, with Swiss Cheese
on Whole Wheat, and Sliced
Fruits*

Veal Stroganoff
*Tender Morsels of Veal in a
Rich Brandy Cream Sauce*

Vegetable Fajitas
*Warm, Soft Tortillas Served with
Onions, Peppers, Pico de Gallo,
Fresh Guacamole, Sour Cream
and Cheese*

CHILDREN'S CHOICE
Beach Burger
The Fun Dog
Peanut Butter and Jelly Sandwich
Chocolate Cake

DESSERTS
Strawberry Banana Mousse
Apple Hollander
Ice Cream
Vanilla, Chocolate, Strawberry, Butter Pecan

Lemon Meringue Pie
Chocolate Gateau
Sherbet
Orange, Pineapple, Lime

BEVERAGES
Freshly Brewed Coffee: Regular or Decaffeinated Iced, Hot and Herbal
Teas, Milk, Skimmed Milk, Hot Chocolate

Carnival Cruise Line Luncheon Menu

RADISSON SEVEN SEAS CRUISES

DINNER MENU

Appetizers

Tequila Shrimp *Gulf Shrimp Flamed in Tequila, Citrus Butter Sauce*
Baked Brie *Wrapped in Phyllo, Topped with Brandied Pecans*
Smoked Pacific Salmon *Tomato, Red Onions, Capers, Bagel, Horseradish*
Escargot *Sauteed with Garlic, Tomato and Cognac on Angel Hair Pasta*
Shrimp Cocktail *Gulf Shrimp with Cocktail and Dijon Mustard Sauce*
Chicken Breast *Wrapped in Phyllo and Herb Cheese, Chive Cream Sauce*

Soups

Corn and Crabmeat Chowder *Scented with Chardonnay*
Pheasant Consomme' *Morel Mushrooms and Vegetable Jardiniere*
Lobster Consomme' *with Fresh Truffles*
Soup of the Day *Prepared Fresh Daily*

Salads

Diamond Salad *Mesclun of Greens, Herb and Champagne Vinaigrette*
Caesar Salad *Hearts of Romaine, Warm Croutons, Caesar Dressing*
Spinach Salad *Fresh Spinach, Wild Mushrooms, Warm Bacon Dressing*
Tomato Salad *Marinated Homegrown Tomatoes, Red Onions, Fresh Basil*

Seafood

Pacific Salmon *Herb Roasted, Pinot Noir Sauce*
Swordfish *Grilled, Tomato Basil Beurre Blanc*
Gulf Shrimp *Grilled, Black Bean Compote, Avocado and Tomato Relish*

Poultry

Chicken Breast *Pan Roasted, Walnut and Smoked Ham Compote*
Duckling *Sauteed Breast of Duck, Peach Pecan Chutney*
Pheasant *Pan Roasted, Wild Rice, White Zinfandel Thyme Sauce*

Steaks and Chops

New York Strip Steak *Grilled, Horseradish Pistachio Butter*
Filet Mignon *Grilled, Green Peppercorn Butter*
Veal Chop *Grilled, Brandied Wild Mushrooms*
Lamb Chops *Pan Roasted, Fresh Mint Pesto*

RADISSON SEVEN SEAS CRUISES
DINNER MENU (cont'd)

Desserts

Chocolate Pate' *A Rich Chocolate Loaf studded with Macadamia Nuts, White Chocolate and Cookies. Served on Raspberry Coulis.*

Gingersnap Tulipe *A Crisp Cookie filled with White Chocolate Mousse and Fresh Berries. Served on Grand Mariner Scented Creme Anglaise*

Sorbet Trio *Tastings of our Homemade Raspberry, Peach and Lemon Sorbets*

Fresh Berry Gratin *Hazelnut Crust filled with Fresh Seasonal Berries. Topped with Champagne Sabayon*

DIET-CONSCIOUS TRAVELERS

Here's a few of the enticing selections, promising to tempt the palate of even the most discriminate dieters.

FISH

A tender salmon fillet, grilled to perfection in apricot-lemon marinade, and served with fresh vegetables and rice or pasta.

SEAFOOD KEBAB

Succulent prawns and swordfish cubes skewered with chunks of pineapple and cherry tomatoes, marinated in herbs, then grilled and served with rice.

BEEF

A rare beef tenderloin fillet served on a bed of assorted greens and vegetables, and tossed with an exotic oriental sesame dressing.

CHICKEN

Boneless chicken strips lightly stir-fried with fresh vegetables and ginger, and served with rice.

PASTA

Fresh pasta tossed with tomato sauce, herbs and pine nuts.

Once on board, if you'll look through the information packet in your stateroom, you'll find this special menu. If not, ask for it in the dining room.

No matter whom you talk to about cruises, probably the first thing they talk about is the food. The food aboard cruise ships is fantastic! We were able to get a "fact sheet" of one year's supply of food for a major cruise ship of 1,000 passengers. This is their **Culinary Fact Sheet.**

❖❖❖❖❖❖❖❖

Caviar—600 pounds. When you say it quickly, it doesn't seem like a lot of food for one entire year. But caviar is not a food, but rather an "experience." Either you love it or you hate it.

Fresh Fish—75 tons. Can you identify with that figure?

Shrimp and Crab—45 tons.

Lobster—50 tons.

Beef—105,000 tons.

Lamb, Pork, Veal—85,000 tons.

Chicken—50 tons.

Milk—115,000 gallons.

Below are the additional foods consumed on the 1,000-passenger ship in a single year (give or take a ton or so of each item).

International cheeses—65,000 pounds.

Fresh Vegetables—570,000 pounds.

Fresh Fruit—600,000 pounds.

Turkey and Ducks—48,000 pounds.

Bacon—21,000 pounds.

Ice Cream—35,000 gallons. Blue Bell Creameries calculated that you get 80 scoops from 3 gallons of their ice cream. That is almost a million scoops of ice cream served per year.

Butter—120,000 quarter-pound sticks of butter. That's 30,000 pounds or 15 tons of butter.

Fresh Eggs—600,000. That means that over a half million chickens cooperated to fill this amount. It brings to mind the joke when you compare eggs with ham. "The chicken is involved . . . whereas the pig is committed!"

The kitchen, "Galley" to you nautical people, is supervised by the Executive Chef, two *sous (assistant) chefs* and a host of *chefs de parties* (cooks). Most food is prepared, on board, DAILY! All pastries, breads, rolls and deserts are made fresh DAILY!

We do not have the figures on the *amounts* of wine and spirits that are consumed because it depends whether more Irishmen, Italians, Frenchmen, Englishmen or Americans traveled that year. We can, however, tell you what is available.

---

35 brands of wine from all over the world

12 brands of champagne

90 brands of whiskey's, spirits and liqueurs

12 brands of beer

8 brands of soft drinks

The typical ship of 1,000 passengers employs over 170 helpers to handle the bars and restaurants. For the dining room alone, they have over 70 waiters, 30 bus boys, 6 wine stewards plus the *Maitre D's* and their assistants.

There are . . .

50 different menus

4 different breakfast menus

1 light menu

50 appetizer selections

120 main courses

70 homemade soups

120 types of bread and rolls

240 desserts

Remember, you are scheduled to eat 12 times a day (give or take a time or two). On these cruises, most people eat until they have to be *stepped on* to help digest their meal.

Chapter 5

CRUISE LINES AND THEIR SHIPS

Before we get into the ships themselves, let's talk about how ships are rated. Why one is four star and another five star? Why you can travel on one ship for $100 a day and another at $2,000 a day? Even though many travel to similar ports what makes one cruise ship better than the other and how can they justify what they charge?

HOW SHIPS ARE RATED

There is a *rating system* for cruise ships, a point system to arrive at this rating that covers, literally, everything! This rating system takes into account the year the ship was built, the maintenance inside and outside the ship and the total cleanliness and hygiene. It includes: the condition of the hull, decking, exterior paint, swimming pool, furniture, lifeboats, public restrooms, elevators, stairways, doorways, passageways, the galley, food preparation, refrigeration, handling, incineration and waste disposal.

Every permanent fixture on that ship is evaluated and gets as nitpicky as to cover direction signs, considers ventilation, air conditioning, lighting, degree of crowding for embarking and disembarking passengers, food lines, dinner seating, beds, bedding, paneling, art work, the health facilities, saunas, running tracks, even the quality and amount of writing paper and postcards in the cabins; laundry, flowers, and the size and thickness of the bath towels.

The food is high priority. They evaluate preparation, portions, creativity, variety, appeal, taste, palatability, freshness, balance, color, garnishes and decorations. It takes into consideration the soups, salads, cakes, the wine list and the price range. They inspect the china, silverware, and kitchen cutlery.

This evaluation takes in the overall entertainment program as well as the stage itself, the seating and the seating arrangement, the movie theater, the lectures and special interest programs, the cabin service as far as speed and accuracy that your in-cabin meals are delivered and the overall "feel" and hospitality of the entire staff. It's worse than an inspection at any of the military academies. A five star plus rating (☆☆☆☆☆+) means that everything must be perfect.

The lowest rated ships in this book are all three star plus, most are four stars and above. Whichever of these ships you choose, you'll be treated well. The facts are, that any given day, an extremely slight imperfection might cost the loss of a few points here and there. All the ships we've listed are first class ships with top rated crews.

We've chosen not to list every cruise line in the world; we think it would only confuse you. And, we haven't room to talk about each ship of the cruise lines we have listed. We have, however, listed many of the ships on which we have personally sailed or received outstanding reports on from critics who have sailed on them.

Your travel agent will have color brochures and more information on these ships as well as current prices and itineraries. Since we're listing these cruise lines alphabetically, let's begin with . . .

AMERICAN HAWAII CRUISES

This cruise line travels only the Hawaiian Islands but has an air supplement program from more than 100 gateway cities of the United States. They now have a single ship, the *S.S. Independence,* that is known for its roomy cabins and spacious public areas, highly reminiscent of the glory days of transatlantic ocean liners.

This ship was built in 1951. In 1993 it was refurbished at a cost of $50 million. It visits five ports and four islands in just seven days, traveling from Honolulu (Oahu)

S.S. INDEPENDENCE

past Molokai, to Kahului (Maui) then to Hilo and around the island to Kona (Hawaii), on to Nawiliwili (Kauai) and back to Honolulu.

The ship is large, 682 feet long and 89 feet wide, with a crew of 315. There are 420 total cabins including 55 suites. They sail at night, so passengers have full days to explore Hawaii's crystal blue waters, majestic waterfalls, steaming volcanoes, emerald rain forests, pristine white beaches, colorful coral reefs, quaint villages and historic landmarks.

Dining is casual dress and the food is your choice

of American, Hawaiian or Oriental.

Prices for the 7-day cruise begin at $1,145 per person, two to a cabin. A 3rd or 4th guest may travel in the same cabin for $695 each. Children under 18 years of age may travel with two full-fare passengers for $195 each. One of the not-so-hidden expense is an $85 per passenger port charge. They seldom discount their prices but a recent ad had them offering two nights at a hotel in Hawaii free.

The fares include accommodations, onboard meals, activities and entertainment. All cabins are air conditioned and roomy with wall-to-wall carpeting, private bathroom, shower and one or more closets.

If you want to extend your vacation in Hawaii, you'll save (usually) if you book your hotel through the cruise line.

CARNIVAL CRUISE LINES

Ready for a really good story? It's the history behind one of our more favorite cruise lines, Carnival. We've both traveled on their ships and have nothing but praise for their entire operation.

In 1972, Carnival owned its first ship, the *Mardi Gras*. On her first cruise, the *Mardi Gras* ran aground outside her port in Miami. In its first season, the *Mardi Gras* had to empty the slot machines in the ship's casino to help purchase fuel to return to its home port. Now, Carnival is one of the leaders in the cruise industry.

The *Mardi Gras* has since retired, but Carnival's new fleet includes the *Celebration, Ecstasy, Fantasy, Holiday, Imagination, Inspiration, Jubilee, Sensation,*

Tropicale, and their newest, the *Carnival Destiny,* the largest ship in the world to date, even larger than the QE-2. The *Carnival Destiny* is 101,000 gross registered tons, 892 feet long, and boasts a cruising speed of 21 knots. It carries 2,642 passengers and a staff of 1,100.

DESTINY

The Destiny will operate a year-round schedule of 7-day cruises from Miami, alternating weekly to the Eastern and Western Caribbean.

Carnival's quality contemporary experience is your best vacation value and means fun and relaxation for all ages. New *Fun Ship Cruises* of from 3-7 days sail from Miami, Port Canaveral, New Orleans and Tampa. A great value! Carnival travels to Mexico, the Eastern, the Western and the Southern Caribbean, the Bahamas, Alaska, Hawaii and the Panama Canal. Their officers are Italian and their service staff is International.

Carnival has many specials and discounts for individuals and for groups and discount substantially off their brochure price *if booked early.*

A terrific feature of Carnival ships is their on board children's camp called **Camp Carnival**, especially created for parents who bring their children.

Prices for a cruise aboard a Carnival ship (not counting airfare) is in the $100 per person, per day  price range. Often, they feature *unbelievable* specials.

CELEBRATION

A recent one was aboard *Celebration* that embarks from New Orleans on a 7-day Caribbean venture with prices starting at $560. Aboard the *Celebration,* there is constant fun with almost 1,500 passengers. The *Celebration* has a wide range of activities and entertainment for everyone on their first cruise. We are showing a few of the Carnival ships and have no favorite; they are all beautiful. More than the beauty is the FUN these ships offer. The photo below is of the SuperLiner, *Fascination*, being greeted by a water-squirting tug boat as she arrives at San Juan Harbor in Puerto Rico. The 70,000 ton, 855 foot, 2,040 passenger

FASCINATION

luxury liner departs every Saturday on 7-day cruises from San Juan to the Southern Caribbean ports of St. Thomas (US Virgin Islands), Guadeloupe (French West Indies), Grenada (the Lesser Antilles) to La Guaira/Caracas (Venezuela), and Aruba (Netherlands Antilles).

The *Fascination* features the seven-story, glass *Grand Atrium Plaza*, the elegant *Beverly Hills Bar*, and the tropical ambiance of the *Coconut Grove Bar & Grill*. The food served in their *Sensation Dining Room* (no smoking allowed) will make you never want home cookin' again.

You can't miss their three-deck-high glass enclosed health spa and gym, the lavish multi-tiered showroom, or their gigantic gambling casino. The original cost of this vessel was $315 million. It has 10 decks and a crew of 920. A fun vacation? Never doubt it!

CELEBRITY CRUISES

Anne Campbell, author of *Fielding Cruises 1995*, writes, "Celebrity is an all five-star fleet . . . its cuisine, service and decor among the finest afloat."

Travel Trade magazine describes a cruise on a Celebrity ship as, "Elegant, yet with a casual touch, sophisticated without glitz or neon. Traditional yet with contemporary influences."

Fordor's Cruises and Ports of Call 1995 also talks about the cuisine on Celebrity. "In terms of quality and presentation, Celebrity's cuisine is among the best afloat."

The *Berlitz Complete Guide to Cruising* says, "The only major cruise line in the premium market to be awarded five stars for its fleet."

And *we* say that their ship, *Century*, is the Fun Factory headquarters for kids. *Century* features a popular Family Cruising Program, specially designed for three age groups (2-7; 8-12; 13-17) and closely supervised by trained counselors and staff. Most quotes from nationally recognized travel magazines talk about the food and we like that, don't we? But other than the food, the entertainment is also superb, from the comedians and brightly costumed dancers to song-filled reviews. There's still dancing to the big bands, a visit to the casino or

maybe some disco dancing. Or perhaps just a stroll around the deck or maybe the midnight buffet? After thinking about it, the consensus of opinion is, "Let's do it all!"

Celebrity travels to the Caribbean for 7, 10, & 11-night cruises aboard. Their ships, the *Meridian, Horizon, Zenith* and their newest, the *Century.*

The *Century* made its debut in December of 1995, a truly breathtakingly beautiful ship with 875 total cabins and a crew of 843 and an unbelievable space ratio of 40! Their 10-night cruises begin in San Juan, and go to Aruba, La Guaira, Grenada, Barbados, St. Lucia, Martinique, St. Maarten, St. Thomas and on to Ft. Lauderdale. Prices, per person, two to a cabin, start at $1,845 (*including* air from over 100 major cities in the US) and there are early booking discounts.

Celebrity ships are easy to recognize with their large X painted on the Funnel (looks kinda like a smokestack) of their ships. The X is the Greek letter "C" that stands for *Chandris*, their parent company.

Two of the Celebrity fleet, *The Horizon* and *The Zenith*, are among the top rated cruise ships in the world. The *Galaxy* at a cost of $320 million, is 73,850 tons with a passenger capacity of over 1,800, makes her debut on December 18, 1996 and will travel from New York to Bermuda for 7-day treks, and from Los Angeles to San Juan *via* the Panama Canal. The Officers are Greek and the service staff is International.

Yet another ship, the *Constellation,* at a cost of $320 million, same size as the *Galaxy*, will enter the fleet in November of 1997.

COSTA CRUISES

Cruising *Italian style* is Costa. It's unlike anything you've ever experienced. Basking in the warmth of Costa's Caribbean on a ship reflecting the beauty of Italy. The stunning *CostaRomantica* or elegant *CostaAllegra* were created by the most progressive design studios in Italy—in the world!

COSTA ROMANTICA

The *Costa Romantica,* 56,800 tons, 10 passenger decks and a crew of 650 for 1,356 passengers, sails the eastern and western Caribbean for 5-8 days per voyage.

A ship, no matter how painstakingly planned, is only as gracious as its people. On Costa, you're sure to meet the friendliest crew, from pleasant waiters to an attentive stateroom staff who believe in efficiently tending to your needs. It's Costa's Italian heritage that sets Costa apart from other cruise lines and their unique shipboard style that keeps guests coming back cruise after cruise. This is the cruise line to "let yourself go" and prepare for a wonderful time *Cruising Italian Style.* Costa has a large fleet of beautiful ships; the

COSTA ALLEGRA

CostaAllegra, CostaClassica, CostaMarina, CostaPlaya, CostaRomantica, CostaVictoria, Daphne, EugenioCosta

and the *CostaRiviera*. We've both sailed with Costa and received all that the brochure promised—and more! Our experience with Costa cruise ships is that they are warm and friendly, and their prices are highly competitive. The price of a 7-night trek on the *CostaRomantica* and *CostaAllegra* starts at $1,980 per couple! But, if you take advantage of their 90-day early booking (*Adiamo)* rate which reduces it as much as $600, it comes down to less than $100 per day, per person—not including air. That's for your "Italian floating hotel," entertainment, and scrumptious food. A BARGAIN!

COSTA VICTORIA

Costa ships are very popular in Europe and have highly competitive prices. Here's a shot of the *Costa Victoria,* the results of $350 million that gave out 74,000 tons of super luxury with 14 decks, a crew of 780 and if all berths are filled, 2,250 (usual passenger capacity 1,950.)

Costa's newest ship, as yet unnamed, will debut in June of 1997 for another healthy price tag of $350 million and almost 80,000 tons.

CRYSTAL CRUISES

We both love the people and the operation at Crystal Cruises. Our personal experience has been that every one of their employees are eager to please. Our front and back cover photos are from Crystal Cruises. They have two ultra luxury ships. Their *Crystal Symphony*

CRYSTAL SYMPHONY

CRYSTAL COVE on the SYMPHONY

and *Crystal Harmony* are truly superb vessels. Both are

about 50 thousand tons, almost 800 feet long, and carry 960 passengers and a crew of over 550.This line has just been awarded an unprecedented SIX ☆☆☆☆☆☆star rating by *Fielding* and considered to be one of the best cruise lines in the world. Berlitz has both ships rated in

CRYSTAL PENTHOUSE

the top eight cruise ships in existence! The *Crystal Harmony,* takes worldwide cruises and the *Crystal Symphony* travels to Alaska, Australia, southeast Asia as well as the Caribbean at certain times of the year. These ships cost from 240 to 300 million dollars! One book describing the *Crystal Harmony* says, "This ship has just about everything for the discerning seasoned traveler as far as good style, space, comfort, and the facilities of a large vessel capable of voyages of any duration. These ships are, without a doubt, outstanding examples of the latest style in contemporary grand hotels afloat and provide abundant choices and flexibility." The ship is staffed with Scandinavian officers and a European service staff. (Passenger to space ratio 52.2.)

Just over 50,000 tons that spoils 960 passengers

with a crew of 530 and a superb example of a true *luxury* ship.

Christened by Mary Tyler Moore, the *Crystal Harmony* features 260 balcony cabins and each cabin has a TV, VCR, spacious rooms with goose-down pillows and bathrobes and bathtubs in each cabin as well as two hair dryers, individually controlled thermostats, personal in-room safes, a refrigerator and mini-bar. The cuisine is gourmet, the service is excellent and the menus prolific; two sittings for dinner. There is a Hollywood movie theater showing latest movies, a huge show lounge, piano bar, disco, classical entertainment and a casino with Blackjack, Roulette, Craps, Baccarat and slots.

CAESAR'S PALACE

CRYSTAL HARMONY

For the fit and/or sports minded, an indoor/outdoor pool, jacuzzis, swim-up bar service, a complete health club with the latest equipment, aerobic classes, men and women's sauna, a paddle tennis court and a regulation size golf driving range. Naturally, there's shuffle board, table tennis, and a jogging track plus an all-around promenade deck for those who love to walk.

These photos, as superb as they are in black and white, simply don't do justice to these magnificent luxury vessels. Rush to your travel agent for a color brochure and dream about your next vacation with Crystal Cruises.

SEAHORSE POOL on the HARMONY

For January of 1997, look for "Voyage of the Hemispheres" World Cruise

PALM COURT on the HARMONY

aboard the elegant *Crystal Symphony.* It will begin in Los Angeles January 17th for a 103-day, five continent in four hemispheres and end on May 1st, in Ft. Lauderdale. And, as usual, guests will savor the world-class cuisine, a rich variety of award-winning onboard entertainment including the expertise of the most prominent and personable lecturers in the world.

For those who like to "visit" a place, this world cruise will make two-and three-day port visits sprinkled in their itinerary with ports along the west coast of Australia, the east and west coasts of Africa and the west coast of South America into the Caribbean. This "world cruise" is also offered in segments ranging from 16-25 days for those who cannot make the entire voyage.

For the days at sea, lecturers and celebrities offer fascinating presentations including former Defense Secretary Caspar Weinberger and Wolfgang Puck, owner/chef of Spago restaurant in Los Angeles, former museum director Thomas Hoving, author John Jakes and artist Guy Buffet. As of this writing they are planning famed lecturers from the worlds of politics and the arts, cultural studies, economics, cuisine, natural sciences, sports and technology to be aboard to share unique insights on local, global and historical issues.

Fares for the full 103-day World Cruise start at $40,830 per person and segment cruises begin at $7,995 per person. Fares include air transportation to and from the cruise destinations.

Crystal Cruises recognizes the fact that single travelers may not want to share a cabin so they have introduced low single supplement rate for the sole use of a stateroom. In 1996, travelers pay only 15% more than the per person, double occupancy fares for private use in some of their staterooms, including deluxe staterooms with verandahs on the luxurious *Crystal Symphony* and *Crystal Harmony*.

Also in 1996, Crystal Cruises offers 6-to 96-day itineraries spanning the globe to spots like Mexico, the South Pacific, the Orient, the Mediterranean, Scandinavia, Russia, the Panama Canal, the Caribbean and Alaska.

There are also **super specials** on Crystal such as trips for $300-400 per day per person to anywhere in the world, including airfare. Plus, Crystal Cruises sometimes has specials (*Harmony Fares*) if you can travel any time of year. Do yourself a favor, go immediately to your travel agent for color brochures and more information on Crystal Cruises.

CUNARD CRUISE LINE LIMITED

According to the *1996 Berlitz Complete Guide to Cruising*, their rating system gives Cunard ships three in the first four as tops in the industry—five PLUS ☆☆☆☆☆+ star rating. They give Cunard's most famous ship, the *Queen Elizabeth 2* (QE-2) *Grill Class* a ranking of but five stars, possibly because she is getting "up in age." We feel the story of the *Queen Elizabeth 2* is worth telling; it's perhaps the most famous ship in all the world. Yes, let's talk about the QE-2. If money is no object, we think everyone should take a trip aboard the QE-2. You may choose a 5-day Transatlantic crossing or a Caribbean, Europe and World cruise. This magnificent "hotel of the sea" was christened by Her Majesty, Queen

Elizabeth II, on May 2nd of 1969.

The QE-2 is big, almost 1,000 feet long and is just over 105 feet wide. She has 13 decks, a crew of just over a thousand and carries 1,800 passengers. The QE-2 is the only regularly scheduled Transatlantic liner in service. At this time, she's the fastest at 30 knots per hour with almost no vibration at the stern.

QE-2

The QE-2 is like a large "city" at sea and like any city, there are several parts of town. There are three distinct classes; the best, the *Grill Class,* has 424 beds and penthouse suites with butler service, and diningis in one of the following three rooms; *Queens Grill, Britannia Grill* and *Princess Grill* (☆☆☆☆☆).

The *Deluxe Class* with 558 beds are outside double cabins and inside and outside single cabins. Your food is served in the Coronia Restaurant (☆☆☆☆).

The *Premium Class* feature cabins for 910 passengers and two-seating dining in the *Mauritania* Restaurant; (☆☆☆) rating. Except for the most serious gourmet, three stars is far better food than most meals you'd ever get at home—even if grandma cooked them.

Grill and *Deluxe Class* have a separate deck and assigned chairs (for an extra fee) but you must sit with all other passengers for major shows, other entertainment events, and social functions.

On most of the other cruise ships, a person can get the smallest inside cabin at the far either end of the ship and yet still frequent any and all other parts of the ship. The food's the same, the entertainment's the same and the itinerary is the same; the only difference is the size of your cabin and the amenities therein.

> If you are budget conscious or could care less what people think, get the least expensive cabin available.

The QE-2 has a special Cunard/British Airways *Concorde* program that is wondrous. On the *Concorde* you fly one way in three hours and fifteen minutes from New York to London (or vice versa) and on the QE-2, five days back. It is not only an adventure few have taken but an experience all should consider. The officers are decidedly British, and the service staff is both British and International.

> We haven't talked about taking pets on board a cruise ship. The QE-2 has 16 air-conditioned kennels for dogs, cat containers, and special cages for birds. It's less expensive to hire a pet sitter while you're away.

The QE-2 also has room for 40 automobiles in the event you want to drive your own car.

ROYAL VIKING SUN

The world's outstanding luxury cruise line includes not only the fabled *Queen Elizabeth 2* but also the largest Five-Star plus fleet. It travels everywhere! Let's talk about a few of these great ships. Their fleet includes, the *Cunard Countess, Cunard Dynasty, Queen Elizabeth 2, Royal Viking Sun, Sea Goddess I, Sea Goddess II,* and the *Vistafjord.*

The *Royal Viking Sun. Berlitz* has it as the top ship in the world and is ☆☆☆☆☆+. It is 675 feet long, 91 feet wide and holds 750 passengers and a mostly European crew of 460. It has a casino, two swimming pools, sauna, steam room, whirlpools and gymnasium, movie theater, a wraparound promenade deck and features excellent cuisine with a menu that is never repeated regardless how long the voyage. The officers are Norwegian and the service staff are European/Asian.

On all the Cunard ships, there is a guest lecture program of interesting speakers and a host program of distinguished male guests for single ladies to dine and dance with who will also escort these ladies on shore tours.

Each cabin aboard the *Royal Viking Sun* has walk-in closets, lockable drawers, full-length mirrors, hair dryers and fluffy cotton bathrobes. Each cabin has a television, a VCR, and 38% of the cabins have private balconies. The *Royal Viking Sun* operates mainly long-distance cruises, including an annual complete world cruise, in maximum comfort. Segments of the world cruise are also available.

Their famous Stella Polaris lounge is one of the most elegant lounges at sea. For golfers, their Pebble Beach is the ship's own golf club, complete with wet bar and electronic golf simulator.

Prices for a voyage on the *Royal Viking Sun* are reasonable. For instance, on one of their sailings called *Voyage Transatlantique*, an 18-day transatlantic jaunt that departs from Quebec that stops in Sydney (Nova Scotia) then across the Atlantic to Cork and Waterford, Ireland, with stops in Amsterdam, Ghent, Belgium, and Honfleur and Rouen (Paris) France, the price range begins under $7,000. Save 20% off of that for an early booking discount. (Again, these prices are not carved in stone because they change; ask your travel agent for current prices, special offers, early booking discounts and trip information).

They also feature a Black Sea/Holy Land cruise that departs Genoa (Italy) with ports of call at Valleta (Malta), Ayios Nicolaos (Crete), Antalya (Turkey), Limassol (Cyprus), Haira (Israel), Alexandria (Egypt), Kantakolon (Greece) and on to Venice, Italy for disembarkation. Prices—under $6,000 per person. This is their air/sea package. Yes, it includes AIR FARE! There are 6, 7, and 8-day segments of this cruise that begin as low as $3,200.

Here is the cost of traveling on Cunard's *Dynasty*

on a Panama Canal cruise on their Air/Sea package for some of the 1996/1997 season. For 10 days, the lowest fare is $1,600 (that's $160 dollars per day!) Their deluxe cabin is a bit over $4,000, just $400 per day.

For an Alaskan trip for 7-days, their fares begin at $160 per person per day also. Again, that's including AIR FARE! There is not a reason in the world that most people in America can't take such a cruise.

RIVER CRUISES

Cunard also has five elegant vessels that sail the great rivers of Europe. Their *Mozart* and *Danube Princess* sail the Danube, their *Dresden* sails the Elbe, their *Prussian Princess* navigates the Rhine. Their *Princesse de Provence*, the Rhone. Prices start at $1,280 for a 7-day cruise.

THE MOZART

The *Mozart* has 204 cabins, The *Danube Princess,* approximately 95 cabins, the *Dresden* shows 54 cabins, the *Prussian Princess*, 69 cabins, and the *Princesse de Provence*, 70 cabins.

Cunard has a package that let's you explore these various parts of Europe before or after your river cruise for three days of First Class hotel accommodations, Continental breakfast each morning, sightseeing tours, transfers to and from the vessel—everything—beginning at $895 per person.

You will find the intimate, European "floating hotels" accented by elegant furnishings, beautifully appointed public areas, and a stunning private art collection. Each vessel's interior has been designed to reflect the unique ambiance of the region through which it cruises.

Just settle into a cozy lounge chair on deck and watch as ancient castles, cathedrals, storybook villages, and magnificent cities appear before your very eyes. On the *Mozart, Dresden* or the *Danube Princess*, there are exercise and massage facilities, a sauna, whirlpools and a heated swimming pool.

And the evening food features romantic candlelight dinners before visiting the intimate lounges and bars for conversation or enjoy chamber music, dancing or local entertainment such as Hungarian gypsy bands or flamenco dancers. Finish off the day with crepes at midnight.

Every morning, a hearty breakfast buffet, mid-morning boullion and delectable five-course luncheons are the rule, followed by the traditional afternoon tea with sweet, delicious pastries.

For the evening meal, savor international gourmet cuisine and local specialties served in one luxurious seating. Dinners (up to nine courses) are prepared by master chefs and of course, a fine selection of vintages from the wine-growing regions along the river. Here are a few itineraries for these river cruises.

In short, Cunard has it all available for you and all you need to do is make up your mind when you're going to travel and for how long, then talk to your travel agent.

What a thrill to (perhaps) take the *Concorde* to London, travel though the rivers of Europe, stay at a hotel for several days and sail back to the United States on the QE-2, all for maybe $7,000 per person.

MOZART	DANUBE PRINCESS
THE DANUBE *Seven-day Cruises* *departing each Sunday.* ROUND-TRIP PASSAU, GERMANY	THE DANUBE *Seven-day Cruises* *departing each Saturday.* ROUND-TRIP PASSAU, GERMANY
Ports of Call Passau, Germany Durnstein, Austria Vienna, Austria Esztergom, Hungary Budapest, Hungary Bratislava, Slovakia Melk, Austria Grein, Austria Passau, Germany	*Ports of Call* Passau, Germany Durnstein, Austria Budapest, Hungary Esztergom, Hungary Bratislava, Slovakia Vienna, Austria Melk, Austria Grein, Austria Passau Germany

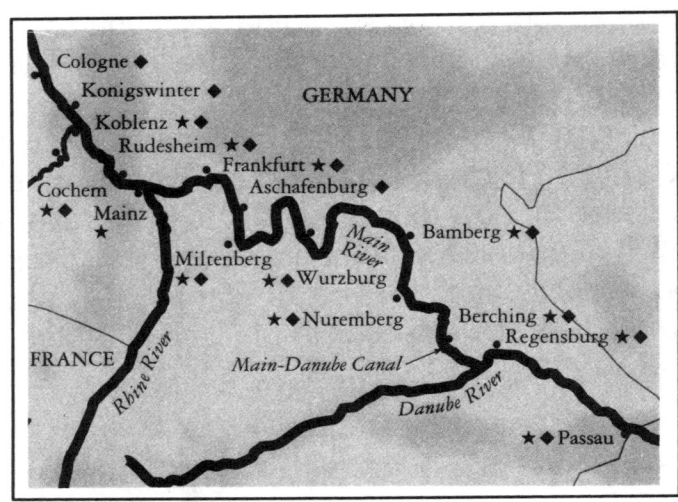

❖ *11-Day Prussian Princess Itinerary* ❖

Frankfurt to Passau

Day	Port	Arrive	Depart
Tuesday	Frankfurt, Germany	——	5 pm
Wednesday	Cologne, Germany	8 am	1 pm
	Konigswinter, Germany	6 pm	7 pm
Thursday	Cochem, Germany	8 am	1 pm
	Koblenz, Germany	6 pm	——
Friday	Koblenz, Germany	——	11am
	Rudesheim, Germany	6 pm	10pm
Saturday	Aschaffenburg, Germany	1 pm	5 pm
	Miltenberg, Germany	11pm	——
Sunday	Miltenberg, Germany	——	1 pm
Monday	Wurzburg, Germany	8 am	3 pm

HOLLAND AMERICA LINE/WESTOURS

There are names like *Maasdam, Nieuw Amsterdam, Noordam, Rotterdam, Ryndam, Staatendam,*

Veendam and *Westerdam.* These are the ships of Holland America. These high-value premium cruises also offer their famous impeccable service, fabulous entertainment and exquisite dining. The Holland America Line has Dutch officers and a service staff of Indonesians and Filipinos who are friendly and thorough.

ROTTERDAM

The *Rotterdam,* Holland America's flagship, and the most famous of all their ships, makes a yearly around the world cruise of 102 days. The majority of her world cruise passengers repeat this trip each year. In 1997, the *Rotterdam* will make her last global trip after much celebration and then leave the Holland America fleet.

To those of you who have traveled aboard the *Rotterdam,* say your last goodbyes to the gracious lady. She will be replaced by the *Rotterdam VI* by August of 1997 which is reputed to be among the fastest ships afloat with a speed of 25 knots, 15% faster on average than today's typical cruise ships. This increased speed enables the *Rotterdam VI* to do such things as add one new port plus four more hours of port time on a typical 10-day Southern Caribbean cruise and add more varied itineraries on its round-the-world cruise. It will hold 1,320 passengers and an entire deck of suites and verandas.

Holland America has been voted the best cruise value from 1992 through 1995 by *Ocean & Cruise News*. Their ships go to Alaska, the Caribbean, the Panama Canal, Europe, Canada and New England. Each year the line takes a "grand cruise" (usually on the *Rotterdam*) and a "round-the-world" cruise. They are one of the most competitive cruise lines in the market.

MAASDAM

The *Maasdam,* and over 1,260 passengers cruise Europe, and make 3, 10-day Trans-Atlantic crossings, the Panama Canal, Caribbean, Alaska and the Western Mediterranean.

Holland America has a fleet of eight ships that are all modern, spacious and luxurious that *Fielding's Worldwide Cruises* rated each ☆☆☆☆☆ vessels. And, Holland America travels to many exotic places you've always wanted to visit but have somehow managed to miss.

They take you to Australia's Outback, the South American rain forest and a trek through the Himalayas. How about a safari in Africa, watch the humpback, beluga and blue wales of the Saguenay Fjord? Or visit Carthage, the Greek Isles, the Holy Land or cruise the European Capitals of Lisbon, Rome, Athens, Paris, Amsterdam, Brussels, and Copenhagen with a tour to St. Petersburg, Russia.

Holland America has been sailing ships for more than 120 years. What an experience it is to travel to parts of the world you've never been to in the comfort, safety and luxury these cruise ships offer.

With its legendary "Tradition of Excellence," Holland America will show you the unspoiled beauty of Alaska while spoiling you along the way with perfected pampering and sumptuous luxury. Your ship is filled with priceless antiques and art treasures valued at more than $2 million. The cuisine is world-class, the service is impeccable, and the seamanship is the legacy of an ancient Dutch tradition. Like royalty in a floating palace, you'll slip gracefully through waters dotted with icebergs and enjoy spectacular deck chair views of majestic glaciers and lovely fjords.

ROTTERDAM & NIEUW AMSTERDAM at the PANAMA CANAL

Holland America moves many of their ships from the Panama Canal voyages to

Alaska from May through September. The *Westerdam*, holds 1,494 passengers, has teakwood outdoor decks and a wraparound promenade deck excellent for sunning and sightseeing. This ship entered the service in 1986 but Holland America, never to be outdone, spent an additional $84 million in 1990 to lenghten it and make it absolutely magnificent. (Holland America has a no tipping policy!)

While touring Alaska with Holland America, don't neglect to look into GRAY LINE, a subsidiary of Holland America Westours that give you a tour through Alaska by boat, train and luxury motor coaches after you leave the Westerdam.

GRAY LINE has an early-and-late-season, 2-day Denali National Park tour for less than $90 per person per day. It originates in Fairbanks and takes you via their luxury glass-domed McKinley Explorer rail cars for a one-night stay in Denali where travelers may then choose an option of river rafting or helicopter flight-seeing. How exciting it would be to go on a river raft tour in Alaska; not many of your friends have done that! Or, take a helicopter ride where the chopper rises and dips along the rivers, between the mountains and you see what few other humans have ever witnessed. It's an experience never to be forgotten.

GRAY LINES also has a similar package that originates in Anchorage and ends in Fairbanks. The tour is one of the best values in Alaska.

NORWEGIAN CRUISE LINES

Their ships cruise the Caribbean, Bahamas, Bermuda, Mexico and Alaska, Their flagship, the *Norway*, at 1,035 feet, is the longest ship afloat that carries almost 2,400 passengers and a crew of 900.

S.S. NORWAY

The *Norway*, originally christened by Madam Charles de Gaulle the *S. S. France* on February 3, 1962 and renamed the *Norway* on June 1, 1980, was refurbished in 1993 at a cost of over $60 million. Because of her two glass-enclosed decks atop the ship house and the 135 outside suites and junior suites, it is one of the most highly recognizable ships afloat. Her classic features and plush splendor is an example of grand ocean liners.

If the Norway fills all berths, she will carry almost 2,400 passengers. At nearly 80 tons there is still plenty of room. For many years, she has been the world's largest ship.

Another of Norwegian Cruise Line's beautiful ships is the *Seaward*, which carries 1,240 passengers and a crew of almost 500. NCL's *Dreamward* and *Windward* are similar in size. These ships have Norwegian officers and an International service staff.

A welcomed addition to their fleet is the *Crown Odyssey* of Royal Cruise Line, now called the *Norwegian Crown*, one of the magnificent ships (we think) anywhere!

It is one of the most comfortable, beautiful, friendly ships afloat. We can't do justice to this magnificent vessel in words nor does this photo that we took personally on our last cruise aboard the *Crown* show it's charm.

NORWEGIAN CROWN

On the *Norwegian Crown* for a 7-day sailing to the Western Caribbean, prices start at just under $1,700. For a 7-day jaunt to Alaska, just under $1,600. This *includes* round trip air from most gateway cities and does *not* include your early-booking discount!

Prices for Norwegian Cruise Line voyages are in the $150-$200 per person per day range. This does include air

LEEWARD

fare in their Air/Sea package. The *Leeward* was refurbished in late 1995 and carries 900 passengers and a crew of 400. They take passengers on 3-and 4-day cruises from Miami to the Bahamas, Mexico and Key West with a stop off at their private island in the Caribbean, Great Stirrup Cay.

PREMIER (The BIG RED BOAT)

This is "the" family-oriented cruise line and their *Star/Ship Atlantic* and *Star/Ship Oceanic* travels to the Bahamas, Caribbean and then DISNEY WORLD, carrying about 1,600 passengers each.

ATLANTIC (top) & OCEANIC (bottom)

The *Big Red Boat* offers you the most colorful vacation of your life. The Captain's awaiting you—bring your family. They'll be well-taken care of . . . especially your children. And don't forget your camera. You've never seen water like this. Water the color of emeralds. Lazy days. White, sugary sand and palm trees that stretch toward the sky. Underwater, multicolored Parrot fish. On board, the sparkling lights of Las Vegas. The golden brown peaks of Baked Alaska. And at night, silver pearls spread out to the horizon. The *Big Red Boat* is the most colorful family vacation you'll ever experience.

Not only will a *Big Red Boat* vacation be the most relaxing of your life . . . a *Big Red Boat* vacation is all inclusive. Which means your 3-or 4-night cruise to the Bahamas is included, as well as 3 or 4 days at the Walt Disney World Resort. Family-sized staterooms, exquisite dining, fabulous entertainment, and on land, your hotel accommodations, admission tickets, rental car, airfare—everything.

The *Big Red Boat* is ideal for kids from 2-4 years for stories, sing-alongs, treasure hunts, a character surprise party and more toys and games than they could ever imagine.

Then there's the kids of 5-7 years, for parachute games, their own swimming pool, magic shows, a tour of the bridge and feature roles in one of the ship's productions.

For the 8-10 year olds, balloon volleyball, lyp-sync competition, kareoke, game shows and activities. Poster-making competition, deliver the *Big Red Boat* news via in-cabin TV, so much to do that they will sleep well every night.

For the 11-13 year olds, a welcome aboard tour, a visit from Taz, games like ship trivia, capture the flag, pool Olympics, beach Olympics and beach basketball.

For the 14-17 year olds, a Sail Away tour, dive in the big pool and beach Olympics. Lyp-sync their favorite tunes on stage, snorkeling in the sea, a dance in their own nightclub, a magic parlor, video arcades and ice cream parlors.

If you want to be alone, let's face it, taking the kids on vacation isn't always a vacation. But the *Big Red Boat* offers 24-hour group babysitting and child care service, so while the kids are having fun doing what kids do, grown-ups have fun doing what they like to do. It's a vacation with kids.

The *Big Red Boat* is docked at Port Canaveral.

Day 1: You drive to it in your complimentary rental car, stow your gear and sample the luncheon buffet.

Day 2: Relax by the pool (the kids are playing under close supervision) and you can try the casino, lounge in the sun, enjoy the sunset.

Day 3: See Nassau in the distance and then visit the world's most irresistible straw market and "shop till you drop." Discover Saly Cay where you can swim, snorkel, play volleyball, rest in a hammock, explore hidden coves.

Day 4:   Overnight, you've come to another tropical paradise, Port Lucaya with an outdoor marketplace of 80 shops. Scuba dive, parasail, pet some dolphins. Then, back to the boat for those delicious meals and the sail back to the US.

Day 5:   You've had the time of your life but your vacation's just getting started. Hop into your rental car toward Orlando with first, a side trip to Spaceport USA at the Kennedy Space Center. Your kids will learn and so will you.

Day 6:   A busy day, with your unlimited admission to the Disney themed parks. Bring your camera and lots of film.

Day 7:   The last day of your *Big Red Boat* vacation. Say goodby to your Looney Tunes characters and know that you've experienced the most colorful vacation of your life. The kids loved it too.

The price: Special deals all year long for families and there are 3, 4 and 7-day tours with reservations in different hotels that cause a variation in prices. A 4-night cruise, including airfare, starts at $649 per person. Again, check with your travel agent for current prices.

PRINCESS CRUISES

It was in 1975 when Princess Cruises, who now owns a fleet of the most modern passenger ships in the world, became a household name as "*The Love Boat*" chose Princess ships for their highly successful series. You all must remember the Captain (Gavin MacLeod), Doc, Julie, Gopher and Isaac and a long list of highly successful stars who played weekly roles at sea. Whatever you saw on the "Love Boat" series is typical on Princess ships.

CROWN PRINCESS

Christened by Sophia Loren and carrying almost 1,600 passengers, the *Crown Princess* has a three-deck-high atrium that features a grand staircase with a fountain sculpture. The cabins have walk-in closets and large bathrooms.

From early morning until well after midnight the Princess ships hum with energy. It's the sound of people having fun. It's nonstop activity or total relaxation. It's the passengers choice. There are language lessons, pool games, lectures, movies and relaxing by the pool during the day. By night, music, dancing, casino, lounges, movies and Broadway shows. Let's look at a few more of the outstanding ships of Princess Cruises.

REGAL PRINCESS

Christened by Margaret Thatcher, the *Regal Princess* holds 1,590 passengers and a crew of 700. The *Love Boat* is making several treks to the Caribbean (French Martinique, British Barbados, Dutch St. Maarten, and St. Thomas in the US Virgin Islands) with a day on Princess

Bay, their very own island. And the airfare is included for $1,148 for the complete package.

STAR PRINCESS

Other ships in this *Love Boat* include the *Golden Princess*, 804 passengers; *Island Princess* and *Pacific Princess*, 610 passengers each; *Royal Princess* and *Sky Princess*, 1,200 passengers each; and the *Sun Princess,* the most innovative and newest of their larger ships at a cost of over $300 million and will accommodate almost 2,000 passengers.

Star Princess, christened by Audrey Hepburn, holds 1,470 passengers.

In late 1997, the *Grand Princess* will set a new cruising standard at **104,000 tons**, the first ship in the line's history to break the 100,000 ton mark, with 2,600 passengers, three state-of-the-art show lounges, three separate main dining rooms, and an innovative two-level, 24-hour indoor-outdoor Lido dining restaurant.

Also, a motion-based virtual reality theater, a golf driving range, and a "blue screen" room which will give passengers the chance to star in their own video production.

The ship will include a retractable magradome enclosing the upper pool area in air conditioned comfort, a spectacular nightclub positioned 15 decks above the sea accessible only by a moving, glass-enclosed walkway. In addition, a 14,000-square-foot casino, spectacular health spa with suspended swimming pool, business center, children's playroom and teen club as well as a wedding chapel and 28 wheelchair-accessible cabins. The cost, a mere $387 million! With their new *Dawn Princess* arriving a few months earlier, the cruise line will have the capability of transporting 750,000 cruisers around the world in a single year.

Itineraries include:

The Caribbean	Panama Canal	Mexico
South America	Europe	Alaska
Canada/New England	Orient/Asia	India
Australia/New Zealand	Hawaii/Tahiti	Africa

Prices are in the $100-$300 per day per person range, some, including airfare. There are special discounts available for all *Captain's Circle* members.

RADISSON SEVEN SEAS CRUISES

This cruise line is owned by the Radisson hotel chain, and features their *Radisson Diamond*, a catamaran 420 feet long and 105 feet wide that holds 350 passengers plus crew. Every cabin is a suite. This is an experience in luxury cruising.

RADISSON DIAMOND

Probably with the most innovative design in the cruise industry, this ship with four-stabilizing fins makes motion minimal. Because of the side beam (width) the ship offers outstanding space for passengers. Her *passenger to space ratio* is 57 and the crew of nearly 200 to spoil 350 passengers assures you of excellent service.

The *Radisson Diamond* has an outdoor jogging track, a five-deck-high atrium and glass enclosed elevators, and an underwater viewing area. The two-deck-high dining room has a 270° view over the stern and open seating.

On their cruise this year, select from the Mediterranean, Western Europe or the Baltic Republic voyage and receive *free* round trip airfare from many major cities plus 2 deluxe hotel nights before or after your voyage in Barcelona, London, Stockholm, Lisbon, Athens or Rome.

Radisson recently purchased the *Song of Flower*, a small luxury ship which travels almost exclusively in the oriental market with 172 passengers. *Berlitz,* who has the *Song of Flower* rated as five-star comments, "Outstanding, destination-intensive, yet a relaxing cruise experience, delivered with style."

SONG OF FLOWER

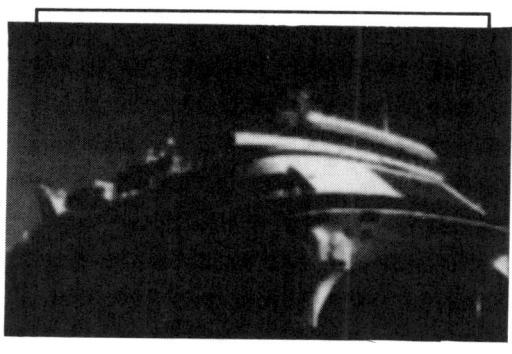

And the *Hanseatic*, that holds 170 passengers, is over 400 feet long and is designed for luxurious adventure cruising. Because of her shallow draft, the *Hanseatic* can access the most remote locales in the world. She is the most luxurious "adventure" vessel in the world to be ice-classed as "1A1 Super," the highest possible rating for a passenger ship.

While on this vessel, they have a fleet of 14 *Zodiacs* that can reach sites others simply cannot. And each cruise has distinguished lecturers to guide you in exploring the pack ice of the Spitzbergen archipelago, the mystical beauty of the Chilean Fjords and view colonies of seabirds nesting along inaccessible cliffs of the Antarctica.

For a 14-day cruise to the Antarctic, Patagonia and South America that includes airfare and 1 night at the hotel Intercontinental Buenos Aires, cabin prices start at $6,675 per person, with an early-booking discount of $500.

The price range is from $200-$600 per person per day on this cruise line depending, of course on the ship and destination. Their officers are Finnish/ American and the service staff, American/International.

RENAISSANCE CRUISES

Renaissance has a fleet of six deluxe ships with names that are easy to remember; *Renaissance III* through *VIII*. Each ship holds about 100 passengers, with a crew of about 72, Italian officers and a service staff that is Filipino and European.

AEGEAN I

The Renaissance ships are not "small boats" by any means; they are all almost 300 feet long with the look of a private  yacht. The *Renaissance VI, VII* and *VIII* carry 114 passengers.

These luxury "small" ships have deluxe outside suites and handcrafted Italian furniture. Each suite has a queen-size bed and a sitting area. All the ships are 4-star ☆☆☆☆ rated.

Dining is in table settings of 2, 4, 6 and 8 persons and there is no specified seating nor set time to eat; sit where you like and eat when you're hungry.

The new Aegean market for Renaissance includes the leasing of a 500-passenger vessel especially for Greek Island cruises with prices that begin as low as $1,995 per person, double occupancy for an inside berth; outside berths begin at $2,495 which INCLUDES air fare and 2 nights stay at a five-star ☆☆☆☆☆ hotel.

Renaissance is taking steps in making this new program *American friendly*. Many Americans don't want to travel on a multinational ship.

Earlier in the year Renaissance announced their entry into the Greek Island cruise program with their 848-passenger leased ship *Marco Polo*. They have included a two-night hotel stay in Istanbul either before or after the cruise in their 9-day package. Also, they have a special program on selected dates for singles with cabin and hotel for just $495 additional.

We like what Renaissance is doing!

ROYAL CARIBBEAN CRUISE LINE

Surely, "the" most magnificent success story of all the cruise lines that offers luxury at a good price. When shopping for a deal and an itinerary, don't neglect asking about Royal Caribbean. Here are some of the reasons.

LEGEND OF THE SEAS

✔Their ships are beautiful, well maintained, and travel (almost) everywhere except South America and the Antarctica. Their itineraries are outstanding and you may choose to cruise for as short as 3 days to as long as forever!

✔They offer the best prices on most cruises, and their ships are large, some carrying two thousand or more passengers.

NORDIC EMPRESS

✔They are considered to be the world's largest cruise line and they are building new ships on a yearly basis. They are innovative in their design of these ships and constantly strive to be top rated; their ships are near the top in everything!

✔They are, pricewise, middle-of-the-market of cruise lines.

As they are proud to say, "Not too many years ago they started with but a single ship." In this case "quality, service and price" had everything to do with their success.

SONG OF AMERICA

✔Their "old" ships are relatively new as far as the cruise industry is concerned and their new ships are breathtakingly beautiful.

Grandeur of the Seas sets sail in November of 1996, at almost 74,000 tons and a passenger capacity of 1,995. As does their *Splendour of the Seas* that entered service in May of 1996 that holds just over 1,800 passengers. Its price tag, $320 million. In early 1997, look for *Rhapsody of the Seas* with space for over 2,000 passengers, *Enchantment of the Seas* in scheduled to appear in April of 1997 and in 1998, they are coming out with *Visions of the Seas,* another super luxury liner of 2,000 plus passenger capacity built by *Chantiers de l'Atlantique* of France.

Already in service, with a remarkable record of passenger satisfaction, is their *Legend of the Seas, Majesty of the Seas, Monarch of the Seas, Nordic Empress, Song of America, Song of Norway, Sovereign of the Seas, Sun Viking and Viking Serenade.*

VIKING SERENADE CROWN LOUNGE

Splendor of the Seas is their newest luxury liner, with soaring glass windows that embrace panoramic views from her seven-story Centrum lobby. Then their splendid the King and I Dining room and Roman Spa, and an 18-hole miniature golf course complete with hills and natural foliage. They are now cruising the British Isles, Europe, and the Orient.

Prices through the Caribbean are approximately $100 a day and their "breakthrough" rates throughout the world, approximately $200 plus per day. Some prices include air. Below are some ideas of the price and the itinerary on board some of these ships.

The *Song of America* departs New York on a 7-day Bermuda cruise for as little as $1,000 per passenger (double occupancy of course). The *Viking Serenade* leaves Los Angeles for 4 nights in Baja Mexico for under $350, and *Splendour of the Seas* cruises for a 12-night Mediterranean adventure with prices that start as low as $3,499 (including air). And yet another 12-nighter to Scandinavia/Russia for $3,699 (including air) and a TransAtlantic trek for 15 nights for less that $3,000.

For updated information as well as any specials

they might offer, consult your travel agent. Royal Caribbean is one of our favorites!

SEABOURN CRUISE LINES

Seabourn is called, "The most celebrated Cruise Line in the world." In fact, it is, according to the travel industry, "The Best of the Best." Experienced travelers concur that "It is the world's best travel experience whether at sea or ashore." Seabourn receives top awards, ratings and honors in authoritative travel and cruise guidebooks and other publications.

This cruise line has three ships, the *Seabourn Pride*, the *Seabourn Spirit* and their newest acquisition, The *Seabourn Legend* (formerly Royal Cruise Line's *Queen Odyssey*). If a person wants to travel in complete luxury (and can afford the price) Seabourn should be their choice.

Seabourn travels to many areas of the world including river cruises. The maximum capacity of the *Seabourn Pride* and the *Seabourn Spirit* is but 204 passengers. The *Seabourn Legend (Queen Odyssey)*, carries 214. It is called, "A most distinguished and upscale cruise line." There are no cabins, only suites.

Their officers are Norwegian, their hotel staff is European and the cruise staff is American/European. And, for these 200 or so passengers, there is a crew of 140. Know in advance that you will be treated better than royalty.

Seabourn is most decidedly "the rich man's cruise line" because they *are* expensive but they offer the best of everything. It's luxury cruising at its finest! Many passengers have booked their cruises back to back; they apparently don't want to return to reality. A special offered for their repeat passengers is a 25% discount for a second cruise, 50% off a third cruise, 75% off a fourth cruise, and the fifth cruise is FREE!

The water sports platform and marina is a fun feature used in suitably calm warm water areas.

Each ship is rated 5 stars plus ☆☆☆☆☆+ with the exception of their new acquisition (the *Seabourn Legend*) which is a few percentage points behind at a solid five star rating. The cruise line will, without a doubt, bring that rating up in a short while.

Fine and unusual dining is a high priority for Seabourn guests. Each evening in their restaurant is an epicurean adventure. Seabourn cuisine has been ac- claimed by restaurant and food writers as not only the finest at sea, but comparable to great restaurants around the world. And there's, open seating; you dine when, where and with whom you choose and, of course, 24-hour room service. For breakfast, you rise as late or as early as you like; you eat when you choose.

The entertainment aboard a Seabourn cruise includes top recording artists; variety shows; jazz, pop, classical, singers, comedians, even magicians and jugglers at times. You may dance in the club or main show lounge or try your luck in the casino. Remember, there is **absolutely no tipping!**

TYPE "A" SUITE

Seabourn's selection of cruises is varied and extraordinary; they travel Southeast Asia, the Orient and India; The Caribbean and Panama Canal; South America and the Amazon; the Mediterranean; the Baltic, Europe and Scandinavia; Africa and the Seychelles; North America: Alaska to Mexico; the South Pacific; the US East Coast and Canada; and "Grand and World cruises" for the blue water sailor from between 25 and 109 days.

On the next page you'll find prices according to suite selections on a few of Seabourn's trips.

Fares are per person, double occupancy and include free economy air travel (USA and Canada), and one night pre-cruise hotel.

14 Days

Seabourn A	Classic Suite B	Regal Suite C	Owner's Suite D/E	Port Fees	Single Occupancy
$12,450	$16,100	$19,800	$21,650	$195	200%

Includes 5 complimentary shore excursions in the Seychelles.

14 Days

Seabourn A	Classic Suite B	Regal Suite C	Owner's Suite D/E	Port Fees	Single Occupancy
$14,950	$19,640	$24,120	$26,360	$ 225	150%

Includes 5 complimentary "Adventure Collection" shore excursions.

14 Days: Istanbul—Haifa
7 Days: Istanbul—Piraeus or Piraeus—Haifa

Seabourn A	Classic Suite B	Regal Suite C	Owner's Suite D/E	Port Fees	Single Occupancy
$14,700	$19,050	$23,400	$25,580	$ 225	125%
$ 8,180	$10,560	$12,940	$14,200	$ 175	125%

SILVERSEA CRUISES

Their *Silver Cloud* and *Silver Wind* are two of the top rated ships in the world, both solid 5-star vessels!

They sail the Caribbean, Europe, the New England Eastern Coasts, the Orient, Southeast Asia, South America and the Antarctic.

These ships carry about 300 passengers, and could best be described as a smaller version of the Crystal ships and a slightly larger version of Seabourn.

SILVER WIND

When you book with Silversea Cruises, you pay for air and the cruise. There is no tipping allowed, it is all included in your package.

In 75% of their suites, there are private teakwood balconies and a teakwood wraparound promenade deck outdoors. Silversea offers special promotions on their cruises. Below are some prices and a few itineraries. You will be pleased with this cruise line, we promise.

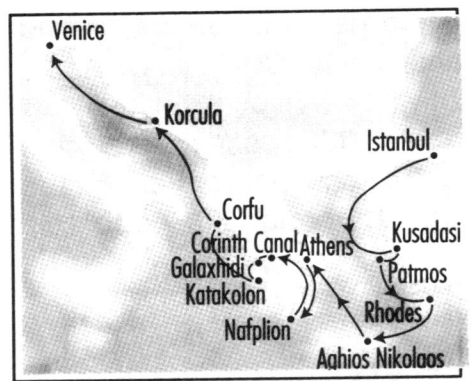

Suites & Prices
Voyage #2619

Suite	7 Day	14 Day
Vista	$5,095	$8,495
Veranda	$5,795	$9,695
Silver	$8,995	$15,045
Royal (1Bdrm)	$9,545	$15,995
Grande (1Bdrm)	$10,445	$17,445
Third Berth	$2,195	$3,645

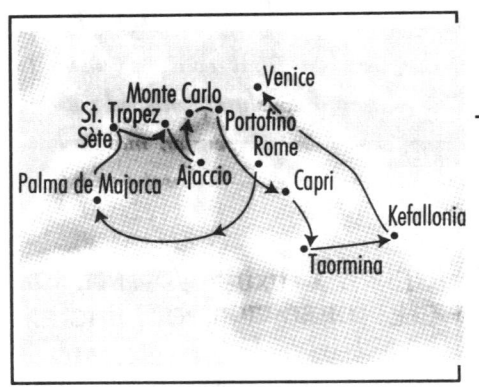

Suites & Prices
Voyage #2622

Suite	7 Day	14 Day
Vista	$5,195	$8,745
Veranda	$5,945	$9,995
Silver	$9,195	$15,495
Royal (1Bdrm)	$9,795	$16,495
Grande (1Bdrm)	$10,695	$17,995
Third Berth	$2,245	$3,745

SUN LINE CRUISES

SUN CRUISE LINE merged with the Greek cruise line, EPIROTIKI, effective December 1st, 1995 with a new name; ROYAL OLYMPIC CRUISES, Ltd. The new combined fleet of six ships: Stella Solaris, 620 passengers; *Stella Oceanis*, 300 passengers; *Odysseus*, 400 passengers; the *Triton*, 670 passengers; *Orpheus*, 300 passengers and *Olympic*, 900 passengers.

Beginning in March of 1996, its first summer of operation, the fleet of ROYAL OLYMPIC CRUISES began their 3-, 4-, 7-, and 14-day cruises to the Greek Islands, Turkey, Egypt and Israel. They also have exciting tours in the Caribbean, South America and the Amazon. They are offering **unbelievable** prices for a 14-day cruise to the "Cradle of Civilization". . . Greece, Turkey, Egypt, Israel and Cyprus aboard the *Stella Solaris* for only $1,940 per person, double occupancy, if you book 60 days ahead of schedule. These fairs run to November of 1996 and if these are successful, there's no doubt this will continue into 1997.

Their *Stella Solaris* recently emerged from Phase III in her 3-year refurbishment program. Everything is fresh and new; carpet, painting, furniture, including her $750,000 Daphne Spa. The *Stella Solaris* will travel the Aegean and Mediterranean from May to October before she sails for Ft. Lauderdale on her annual Exotica West transatlantic cruise to ply the Caribbean, the Amazon River and a few

Panama Canal cruises as well as a voyage to the Land of the Maya. Her home ports will be both Ft. Lauderdale (Florida) and Galveston (Texas).

STELLA SOLARIS

Both Sun Cruise Line and Epiritoki boast of having the friendliest staff, top lecturers and comfortable ships. Their officers are Greek, most of the waiters are Greek and they feature Greek cuisine. These ships are tidy, well maintained and intimate.

Their largest ship is the *Stella Solaris* at 544 feet long with 620 passengers and a crew of 310. Dining aboard is a pleasant experience with Greek waiters and Greek chefs and old-world European service. This ship offers a good price, warmth and comfort.

A "for instance" in price on the *Stella Solaris* from Galveston for a 7-day Caribbean/Mexico cruise is from $726. Great if you live in or around Houston, Texas. They also offer air add-ons at tremendous savings including overnight stays at hotels. Drop in your nearest travel agency and get current brochures, prices and specials on Sun Line and Epirotiki.

WINDSTAR CRUISES

Owned by Carnival (who also owns Holland America and stock in Seabourn) are the *mys Wind Song,* the *mys Wind Spirit,* and the *mys Wind Star.*

The ships of this cruise line are (*mys*) Motor Yacht Sailers, part yacht and part cruise ship with four tall masts and computer-controlled sails. They sail on 7-day cruises with 144 guests to Tahiti, French Polynesia, Caribbean, Mediterranean and Europe.

Treat yourself to luxury in grand style. They cater to snorkelers and scuba divers. You can become certified on board for scuba diving.

Their cuisine is *par excellance*. They recently

hired the services of the famous chef *Jachim Splachal* of Patina and Pinot Bistro of Beverly Hills, who specializes in the top rated nouveau cuisine on these ships. Shirley says it is a culinary delight and has enjoyed the *Wind Song*, the *Wind Spirit,* and the *Wind Star.* "A Windstar cruise is something you will never forget; it's like being on your own private yacht."

WIND SPIRIT

The ship is 440 feet long, with 4, 204 foot masts, a 1,400 kw diesel-electric engine and with comfort, luxury and fine dining.

WIND SONG

440 feet long, 5 decks and a crew of 91 to spoil 144 passengers. 2 kayaks, 2 sunfish sailboats, windsurf boards, water ski boat, scuba and 4 Zodiacs.

BANANA BOAT RIDE

These ships enter ports that larger ships can only dream of entering. For "The Windstar Cruise Experience". Call your travel agent for new, exciting itinerary and current prices.

WINDJAMMERS

These ships are for the true adventurer. They are called "Barefoot Cruises" where informality rules. Yep, it's T-shirts and shorts so trash those tuxedos and ball gowns. It's not exactly "roughing it" but it certainly is different.

You start your day with complimentary Bloody Marys, fresh baked breads and pastries, followed by a bountiful breakfast. Lunch is served either picnic style or on the beach, and dinner is hearty.

When they weigh anchor, the crew does the work. If you choose, you *may* take your turn at the helm and learn the ropes. Do as little or as much as you like. It's adventure aboard a tall ship.

The ships from which to choose include the 282

foot *Fantome,* built in 1927 for the Duke of Westminster. It's among the world's largest four masted stay-sail schooners. Former owners include the Guiness Brewing family and Aristotle Onassis who purchased her as a wedding gift for Princess Grace and Prince Ranier. Onassis was not invited to the wedding and the gift was never delivered.

FANTOME

The crew numbers 45 for 128 passengers and visits St. Barths, St. Kitts, Nevis, Antigua, Montserrat, Guadeloupe, Ille des Saintes, and Dominica in the Caribbean.

FLYING CLOUD

Next, the *Flying Cloud,* 208 feet, a three masted schooner with a crew of 28 and 74 passengers. She has been completely refurbished with modern amenities, stained glass windows and a spiral staircase. She sails like a "privateer" of days of old.

MANDALAY

Queen of the Windjammer fleet is the 236 foot barquentine *Mandalay* built in 1923 for the financier E.F. Hutton. In the 1930's she was sold to shipping magnate George Vettlesen and was later put into service by Columbia University sailing over one and one quarter million miles worldwide.

POLYNESIA

The *Polynesia* is yet another legendary schooner that was built in 1938 and one of the last of the great Portuguese Grand Banks fleet. She is 248 feet long with a crew of 45 and takes on 126 passengers. This exciting ship has all the modern amenities and blends today's comforts with yesterday's romance and grace.

YANKEE CLIPPER

The *Yankee Clipper* is one of the only armor plated private yachts in the world. Confiscated in World War II as a war prize, she was later acquired by the Vanderbilts and renamed *Pioneer.* Racing off Newport Beach, she was considered to be one of the fastest Tall ships on the west coast. In 1965 she joined the Windjammer fleet and was christened, *Yankee Clipper.* She takes on 64 passengers with a crew of 29, is almost 200 feet long and a beam of 30 feet and cruises the Caribbean on 6-day treks.

Amazing Grace explores the Bahamas and Caribbean on 13-day trips with accommodations for 96 passengers and a crew of 40. Built in 1955 at the Caledon Shipyard in Dundee, Scotland, Pharos braved the North Sea delivering supplies to lonely lighthouse keepers and servicing buoys along the coasts of England and Scotland. A "workhorse" vessel, her fine appointments were still elegant enough to play hostess to the Queen of England and the Duchess of York.

AMAZING GRACE

Acquired by Windjammer in 1988 and renamed *Amazing Grace*, she carries on the tradition of old world charm and elegant service with 354 foot length as she island hops between Freeport and Trinidad meeting up with other tall ships, delivering monthly supplies.

Prices on each of these ships begins at just over $108 per day for 6-day cruises and go as high as about $190 per day for the Honeymoon Suite. The low end price is for a bachelor/ette cabin that has six bunks with private head and shower. It is an adventure!

There are discounts on these cruises also, sometimes two for the price of one.

STEAMBOAT RIVER CRUISES

It wouldn't be fair to leave out boats that explore America's heartland as do the 2-to 12-night voyages aboard giant paddle wheel boats that visit 45 ports of call with from 87 to 212 staterooms. Your travel agent will have these brochures. For now, let's talk about them.

DELTA QUEEN STEAMBOAT COMPANY

The Mississippi River spreads up from the Gulf of Mexico, sweeping across North America and reaches far into Canada. The rivers the Mississippi touches are the Ohio, Missouri, Arkansas, Chippewa, Cumberland, Illinois, Ouichita, Red, Tennessee, White and many others.

Since the beginning, man has settled near these waters and traveled the *river highway.* From the Grand Village of the sun worshiping Natchez Indians to the astounding man-made hills of he mound builders, the river banks are dotted with the ruins of Native American cities and ceremonial sites.

As Mark Twain said in **Life On The Mississippi**, *"The steamboats were finer than anything on shore. Compared with superior dwelling-houses and first-class hotels in the valley, they were indubitably magnificent, they were palaces."* . . . and they still are!

AMERICAN QUEEN

Since 1890, the Delta Queen Steamboat Company has proudly served as keeper of America's great steamboat legacy, offering unforgettable Steam-boatin' vacations on the only authentic steam-powered overnight paddle wheelers in the world. Yes, the grandeur and opulence of yesteryear live on, complimented by old-

LADIES PARLOUR

fashioned service and warm hospitality.

The *American Queen* is 418 feet long and carries 436 passengers, 5 decks of opulence, memories and comfort and one to feel the warmth of the southern sun. From all perspectives, the grand *American Queen* is without a doubt, the greatest steamboat the world has ever known. Every detail has been fashioned in the tradition of her palatial predecessors with towering twin smokestacks with fancy "feathered" tops, intricate Victorian fretwork on her elevated pilot house, and a colossal red paddle wheel powered by lovingly refurbished vintage steam engines.To better "tell" of the interior or thismagnificent vessel, look at these photos.

The *Delta Queen* takes you along routes that most Americans think are gone forever. Vast stretches of the river show little sign of the 20th century. You'll see forested river banks, pillared plantation houses and small towns presided over by church steeples that all seem to drift by in slow motion.

DINING ROOM
AMERICAN QUEEN

GRAND
STAIRCASE
MISSISSIPPI QUEEN

DELTA QUEEN

The *Delta
Queen,* was
built in 1926
and designated
a National
Historical
Landmark in
1989. It is 285
feet long and
carries 174

passengers. It is furnished with antiques and high-
quality reproductions that compliment her hardwood

paneling, Tiffany-style transoms and polished brass appointments.

MISSISSIPPI QUEEN

The *Mississippi Queen* is 382 feet long and boasts of being able to transport, comfortably and in grand style, 420 passengers. The three queens take 2- to 14-night cruises through Mark Twain's America. Board her, wave goodby to well-wishers left on the shore and the sound of the calliope—that mighty steam and iron piano—fills the air in salute as the steam whistle sounds and a great red paddle wheel begins to churn and the elegant steamboat gently glides away from the landing and into the river toward the next port-of-call.

"A" SUITE MISSISSIPPI QUEEN

All public areas are completely climate controlled

and each cabin has an individually-controlled thermostat. Rooms are never as large as you like but there's different size cabins and beds that have whatever is necessary to store clothes, bathe and sleep. And the entertainment begins.

Onboard entertainers, stage shows, movies, old-fashioned cabaret, vaudeville, river music and Broadway. The dining, two sittings, is robust Cajun-style and American fare to "Heart Healthy" menus. You'll have Southern fried chicken, New Orleans red beans and rice and roast beef, steak and seafood from the Gulf of Mexico. You'll eat well!

A river steamboat cruise is a grand adventure. Go to your nearest travel agent for color brochures, itineraries and prices.

1996/1997 STEAMBOAT FARES*
Delta Queen, Mississippi Queen, & American Queen

Cruise Length (nights)

	2	3	4	5	6	7	8	9	10	11	12	14
AAA	1230	1840	2420	3030	3620	4150	4750	5340	5890	6470	7070	8250
AA	1030	1540	2040	2540	3040	3480	3980	4480	4990	5540	6060	7070
A	890	1330	1760	2180	2610	2990	3420	3850	4250	4670	5090	5940
B	820	1230	1620	2020	2410	2780	3160	3550	3940	4330	4720	5510
C	750	1120	1480	1840	2210	2530	2890	3250	3590	3930	4290	5000
D	620	930	1220	1520	1820	2070	2370	2670	2960	3250	3540	4130
E	530	790	990	1190	1390	1590	1890	2130	2490	2790	2990	3490
F	330	490	620	740	870	990	1180	1400	1550	1740	1870	—

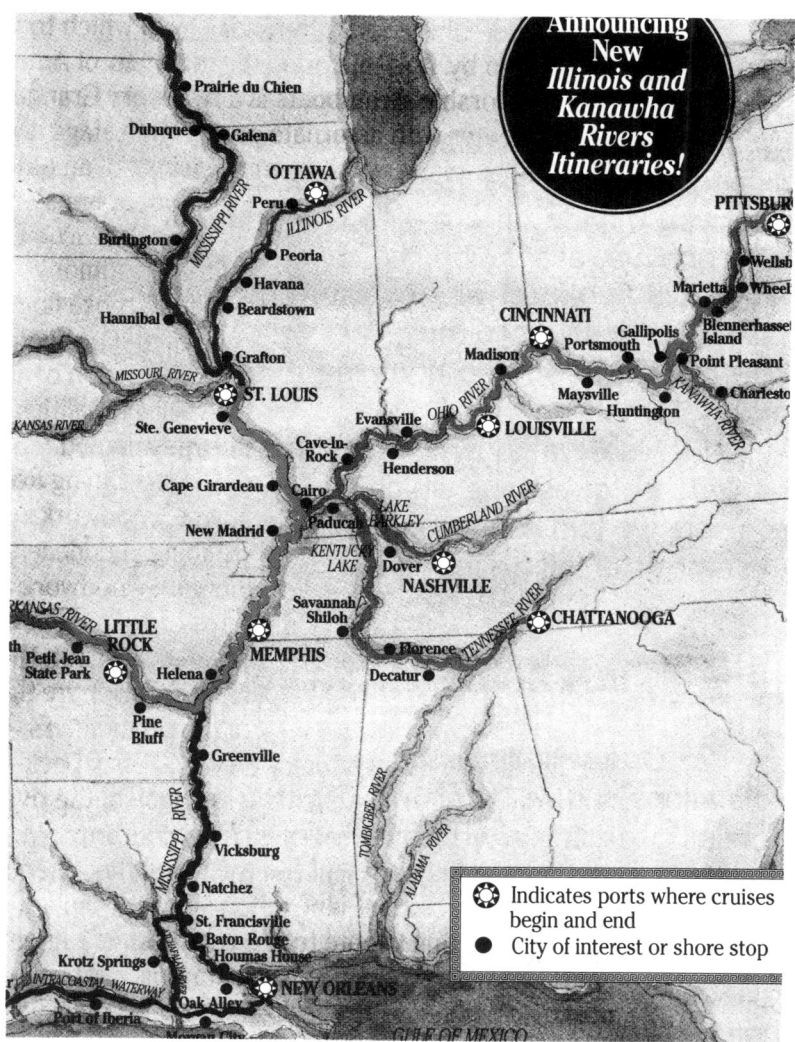

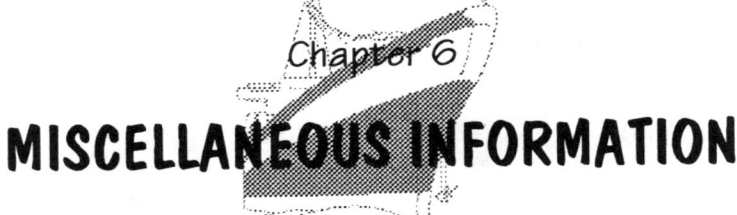

MISCELLANEOUS INFORMATION

First-time cruisers, if you follow what we say in this book you'll do fine. Each cruise line differs slightly and when you decide on a cruise line and talk to your travel agent about a reservation, the cruise line will send you that packet we spoke of earlier with information concerning that particular ship and trip. What we've tried to do is "sell" you on taking a cruise because it is, without a doubt, a fantasy come true.

Also, we know we must have left you with many unanswered questions which we'll attempt to cover now. Let's see, we told you some things about shore excursions but perhaps didn't go into great detail about them. Here's more.

SHORE EXCURSIONS

Cruise ships offer shore excursions at all their destinations and will furnish you with a complete brochure explaining each as well as the price in the information packet they mail to you prior to sailing. Study them carefully and make your selection. Some cruise lines ask that you make your decision and book them before you leave on your voyage. Others ask you to make the choice when on board.

First time passengers usually take all of the shore excursions offered by the ship because they feel safe and want to be "led" everywhere. Smart move, but know that these shore tours can be quite expensive. Make certain they are within your budget.

For those who dare and are unafraid of the unknown, hiring a taxi or rental car or taking a train or bus on your own is oftentimes less expensive, especially if you have another couple to share the expense.

On a recent cruise to Italy, we were forewarned by the Cruise Director that the tour included either Pompeii and the museum or Pompeii and Capri; that it was impossible to see all three. We got with another couple, hired a Mercedes cab, and raced to Pompeii, returned to the port to see the museum, had lunch on board our ship, then took the hydroplane to Capri and still had time to spare. In other words, have fun studying these places by reading about them or talking to someone who has taken this cruise.

For safety and convenience (if you can afford it) the tours handled by the ship are fine. One plus is that you are guaranteed not to be left in a port if there is a mishap on the tour. They will not leave with 65 or 70 passengers short, but if you are traveling as a couple or two couples and you miss the time the ship is to leave for any reason, you will have to catch it at the next port. This can prove to be more expensive than half a dozen tours.

Another plus is that when you purchase a tour from your cruise line, you are fully covered by insurance. On your own, you are not.

For those of you who have cruised before and feel that the cost of a shore excursion is too expensive (of which many are) know that the cruise line rarely makes any (or very little) money from this; it goes to the local tour organizer. The cruise lines go to great expense setting up these various shore excursions through those local operators. They have to staff a Shore Excursion Desk on board, print the information for each tour, guide the tour and handle the problems that arise.

In reading about the tours, take into consideration the words; "see" and "visit". Visit means to remove your body from the transportation and walk into or through a place. Whereas "see" can mean that you fly by at 90 miles an hour and a tour guide points at a palace, cathedral, castle or museum and you have in fact, "seen" it.

WARNING ABOUT TOURS

Some things to be wary of on shore excursions whether you are on your own or on an escorted tour.

✗Pickpockets—Barcelona, Rome, and Rio de Janeiro are some of the "hot spots" for pickpockets. In Rome we were warned against bands of Gypsy youths who surround you, pick and poke and bump into you and steal whatever they can manage. Of all places, the Vatican was where we were confronted by the Gypsy kids who tried to pick our pockets.

Shirley suggests you wear a fanny pack or a small, thin purse that fits *under* your clothes. In some countries you will need your passport; conceal it at all times. There is a huge market for passports and they can be sold easily. Guard your credit cards, cash, and travelers checks.

✗Transportation—In selecting a private car or cab at a port, talk to two or three to get a price, look over to see that the vehicle looks as though it is well maintained, and try to find a driver who speaks your language fluently. It's disconcerting to drive along at a high rate of speed and ask questions without even the faintest hope of an answer. And, do not pay in advance or anywhere along the way or you might be hitchhiking back to the ship. When the trip is over, pay then.

SHOPPING

Be smart when you shop and try not to get something huge or heavy. In Barcelona a year or so back, a friend we met on the cruise bought several of the *Lladro´* glass figurines. They were wrapped delicately and the clerk offered to mail them to his home but the price was a bit much for the postage. But, of the three pieces he brought with him on the plane, two were damaged.

Lladro´, for instance, is usually sold aboard ship at as good (or a better) price than you can get at the factory and they will ship it to your home.

MARRY AT SEA

CARNIVAL CRUISE LINE recently expanded its wedding program to include shipboard services in Georgetown, Cayman Islands, as well as shore side ceremonies on the island. Their ships, *Tropicale*, *Imagination* and *Sensation* have shipboard service for

$225. This isn't the captain marrying you (remember, it's illegal except on Japanese registered ships) but an onboard "marrying person" is available. You get married in their library in a civil ceremony, enjoy a champagne toast in keepsake champagne flutes, flowers for the bride and groom, a small wedding cake, prerecorded wedding music, a decorated bridal aisle, an engraved announcement and marriage certificate suitable for framing and photographic services that include an 8 x 10 portrait.

You can choose to have a ceremony for $675 on Seven Mile Beach in Grand Cayman or a garden service for $750. Grand Cayman requires that you purchase a marriage license there for a cost of $200.

NUDE CRUISES

Yes, there are such cruises "springing up" here and there around the world and one we recently read about in the May 1996 issue of NEW WOMAN magazine written by Maxine Paetro talks about the *Star Clipper*, a 360 foot-long, four-masted tall ship with 100 guest cabins. This voyage begins in Barbados and sails to Tobago, Carriacou, Tobago Cays, Bequia, Saint Vincent and Saint Luciaca in 80° temperature carrying nude passengers (if they so choose).

This particular cruise hosted mostly married couples in their mid-40's, some single couples and some singles traveling alone who just like to "bare it all" and soak up the rays.

You never *have* to be nude," the article read but photos in this article had only nude people, covered but shown. They were all waving and smiling for the camera and "it wasn't a sex thing, no swinging was allowed, it was just a health thing for sun worshipers".

For information pertaining to nude sailings, have fun and ask your travel agent; we dare you! If you are nudists or wannabe's, for nude recreation, call The American Association for Nude Recreation at 1-800-TRY-NUDE. Or The Naturist Society at (414) 426-5009. There is a Bare Necessities Tour and Travel Organization at 1-800-743-0405 or Fax (512) 469-0179.

TELEPHONE or FAX

You will be able to call (or be called from) anywhere on these luxury ships but the cost is rather high; I think it was something like $10-$15 a minute. Our suggestion is to bring your telephone card or credit card and make a call from shore. At most ports there are banks of telephones at that port for you to call home. Your *information packet* will have the telephone number of your ship in the event you need to be reached from your home.

SMALL APPLIANCES

Bring em' along. There are 110 outlets in each cabin. Again, your info packet will tell you.

THEME CRUISES

Yet another program many lines have adopted that have become popular cruises have been those featuring Big Bands, Jazz and other music styles, as well as health and fitness sailings. Many cruise lines feature a team of special guest fitness experts and an abundance of classes and lectures on fitness, nutrition, beauty and emotional and physical well-being.

Some cruise lines have enticed university professors, noted authors, political analysts, art historians, and experts in various fields to conduct on-board special presentations, demonstrations and talks.

These lecturers are absolutely superb and are also hand-picked for sense of humor, quality of information and their in-dept knowledge on their chosen subject.

UNBELIEVABLE DEALS

BEWARE of the unbelievable deals because, "If it's too good to be true, chances are it isn't true!" We've all heard that again and again but still, there are groups "out there" who pose as travel agents and offer unbelievable deals like 4 and 5 day cruises for two for less than $300 per couple. Check this out carefully!

Chances are, you'll be sailing on a scow, packed in closer than cattle and receive minimum service—if any. We've taken one and investigated dozens, so we know what we're talking about! It will be a living nightmare. Go to a legitimate travel agent and look for a deal but not an unbelievable one; they don't exist!

And last but not least, a fun list from Celebrity Cruises of the . . .

TOP 10 WILDEST QUESTIONS PASSENGERS ASK

How will we know which photo is ours?

Will trapshooting be held outside?

What time is the midnight buffet?

Is there water all around the island?

Does the crew sleep on board?

What do you do with the ice carving after it melts?

Will I get wet if I go snorkeling?

Does the ship generate its own electricity?

Does the ship rock only when we're at sea?

Does the elevator go to the front of the ship?

We hope we've tempted you to take a cruise. ALL ABOUT CRUISES is distributed throughout the United States, Europe and the Orient. It can be found in most retail book stores, even on a few of the cruise ships we've highlighted. We are encouraging the better cruise agencies to give them as gifts.

In parting, remember two additional things about cruising. *Never travel without an umbrella or raincoat and . . . avoid whingers!*

PHOTO CREDITS

Andy Newman/CCL, for his photo of the cascading 114-foot-high waterfall on a Carnival ship and to Wieck Photo Database for the shot of Carnival Cruise Lines' Superliner *Fascination* on Page 71.

To Gary Nolton for his Windstar Cruises photo of the *Wind Song* in French Polynesia and to Harvey Lloyd/Windstar Cruises for the *Wind Spirit* photo on the island of Corsica, on page 119. Another Gary Nolton credit for his "banana boat" photo on page 120.

Other photos, slides, and itineraries were either sent to us by the various cruise lines we list earlier in the book or taken from their brochures and sales catalogs.

We'd also like to thank CLIA and GIANTS for their help, as well as *Supertravel* and *Uniglobe*. And to *Mediatel Fax Service* and that fine magazine most travel agents live by, TRAVEL WEEKLY. All of the above kept us apprised of happenings and changes in the cruise industry and were essential to the completion of this book.

Also, Barnes & Noble, Border's, Bookstop, Waldenbooks, B. Dalton and the many independent bookstores around the world that have asked to carry our book . . .

ALL ABOUT CRUISES.

SHIRLEY RAGUSA, co-author of this book, is a *cruise expert!* She has owned a cruise company and served as a cruise advisor to travelers for many years.

Shirley has cruised all over the world on most of the ships afloat, and is extremely adamant in her advice to all who plan to cruise; "Consult with an *experienced* travel agent who knows the cruise line and has either been on that particular ship or knows about exactly what they are recommending."

If you want expert advice, up to date information on cruise lines, their ships and the best prices, give Shirley a call on her worldwide toll-free number. She can answer any question on cruising you might have and will enjoy visiting with you.

Call Shirley: 1-800-700-4170

Other Books by Swan Publishing

HOW NOT TO BE LONELY . . . If you're about to marry, recently divorced or widowed, want to forgive, forget or both, this is an excellent book to read. Candid, positive, entertaining and informative —a fun book to read with answers that will help you get a date or a mate. It tells you where to find them, what to say and how to keep them. (Over 3 million copies sold) . . . . $ 9.95

HOW NOT TO BE LONELY *TONIGHT* . . . The sequel for the *MALE* reader. Other than being courageous and strong, smart women want their man to be sensitive, caring, and understanding. "The" book to give to your man. Or, for men who really want to learn what turns the modern woman on . . . . $ 9.95

NEW FATHER'S BABY GUIDE . . . Another best selling book by Pete Billac. The **perfect gift** for ALL new fathers. There is not a book for new fathers quite like this one! Tells (dummy dad) about Lamaze classes, burping, feeding and changing the baby plus 40 side-splitting drawings by athlete/cartoonist Cash Lambin. Most of all, it tells dad how to **SPOIL** mom! **GET IT** for that new daddy! . . . . $ 9.95

HOW TO BUY A NEW CAR & SAVE THOU$ANDS . . . Inside information on dealerships and salespersons. This book by Cliff Evans, a former car salesman and general manager, really will save you thousands on your next new car purchase . . . . $ 9.95

A WOMAN'S GUIDE TO SEXUAL ENHANCEMENT. . . or **REVERSING IMPOTENCE** *FOREVER* . . . A truly great book written by two world famous urologists, Dr. David F. Mobley and Dr. Steven K. Wilson. This books tells MEN how they can REVERSE this problem but, woefully, men just aren't buying the book. It seems that men feel it's a terrible thing to mention whereas the terrible thing is **not doing anything about it!** The book has many drawings that explains how impotence can be reversed and is **perfect** for the woman to read, then "slip it" under her partner's pillow . . . . $ 9.95

PETE BILLAC, co-author, is one of the most sought-after speakers in the United States. He is billed as an Author/Lecturer/Humorist, and has written 38 full-length books, hundreds of short stories and conducts fun lectures on cruise ships. Perhaps you've seen Pete on Donahue, Sally Jessy Raphael, Good Morning America or any of the other network televison shows.

Pete writes what pleases him, and everything is well researched and humorous. He's penned books on adventure, war, romance, famous people, self-help and animals. He talks to Fortune 500 companies on marketing, schoolkids on reading and writing and to folks over 60 on keeping physically fit and enjoying life. He makes his audiences laugh . . . hard!

Phil Donahue said, "Pete is an expert at restoring self-confidence and self-esteem in others."

Ken Collins, Syndicated Radio Celebrity Host said, "One of the funniest, most charismatic speakers I have ever heard. He breathes life into every topic. Be sure to attend any function where Pete is featured."

SHIRLEY RAGUSA and PETE BILLAC are available for personal appearances, luncheons, banquets, seminars, etc. Call (713) 388-3547 for cost and availabilty.

For each book, send a personal check or money order in the amount of $12.85 per copy to:
Swan Publishing, 126 Live Oak, Alvin, TX, 77511.

To order by major credit card 24 hours a day call:
(713) 268-6776 or long distance 1-800-866-8962
Delivery in 2-7 days

LIBRARIES—BOOKSTORES—QUANTITY ORDERS:

Swan Publishing
126 Live Oak
Alvin, TX   77511

Call (713) 388-2547
FAX (713) 585-3738